CW00957295

The Ideals
and Training
of a
Flying Officer

The Ideals
and Training
of a
Flying Officer

Roderick Ward Maclennan

 Crécy

Crécy Publishing Ltd

First published in England by Crécy Publishing Ltd 2009

Printed in England by the Cromwell Press Group
Designed by Wendy Barratt

ISBN 9 780859 791304

Crécy Publishing Ltd
1a Ringway Trading Estate, Shadowmoss Rd, Manchester, M22 5LH

Roderick Ward Maclennan

Introduction

Roderick Ward Maclennan, known to his friends as Ward, was born in Toronto on the 17th of May, 1893. He entered Queen's University in that city in 1910, as both his father and his grandfather Maclennan were graduates of Queen's and he later decided to follow his father in the legal profession. In October 1914, Ward registered in the Law School at Osgoode Hall. One immediate result of the War was the Osgoode Rifle Club which he joined and he soon became one of the crack shots. Ward completed his first year in law in the spring of 1915, and in October commenced his second, and at the same time joined an Officers' Training Corps connected with the University of Toronto. In December Ward decided to join the reinforcements which Queen's was gathering to send to her Hospital then at Cairo. In January 1916 Ward went to Kingston and enlisted as Private number 03755. While there he received the result of the Christmas law examinations, standing fifth in a class of about 90. In his farewell letter from Kingston Ward said:

> "I wish you all goodbye again, and remember
> that I am going off on work which is
> congenial and necessary, and I could not with
> any self respect stay in Toronto any longer."

He sailed from St. John with the rank of Sergeant on the 2nd of March, crossing the Atlantic on the Scandinavian.

"There was frequent lifeboat drill. When we were within a day or two of England greater precautions were taken. I was chased back to my room by the guard several times, because I had started without my belt. They were carried everywhere, to the dining room, to the lavatories and on deck. It made me think of the Ancient Mariner and the Albatross, to see all the passengers going round with white life preservers slung round their necks. On the ninth day we began steering a zigzag course. On March 12th the "Mosquito fleet" came out to meet us. Away on the horizon to starboard I saw three small black specks, gradually growing larger, racing towards us like mad. Others rushed towards from the port side, and presently we had seven wicked looking torpedo boats escorting us. Flashes from their signal lamps ordered alterations in our course. Presently HMS Drake speeded up and disappeared over the horizon ahead. As we lay in Plymouth harbour I was impressed by the hills, green and brown in the sun, and after snowbound Canada the sight of green herbage was most welcome."

Ward was soon taken on the orderly room staff of the Canadian Army Medical Corps Training School then stationed at Dibgate, a clearing depot for the Canadian Medical Service. In June 1916, Ward was transferred to the Shorncliffe Military Hospital to organize a new staff and in a short time he was advanced to the rank of Staff Sergeant.

Description of Roderick Ward Maclennan **on Enlistment.**

Apparent Age.....22.years....9 8....months.
<small>To be determined according to the instructions given in the Regulations for Army Medical Services.</small>

Distinctive marks, and marks indicating congenital peculiarities or previous disease.
<small>(Should the Medical Officer be of opinion that the recruit has served before, he will, unless the man acknowledges to any previous service, attach a slip to that effect, for the information of the Approving Officer.)</small>

Height..................5..ft...8...ins.

Chest measurement. { Girth when fully expanded...........37..ins.
Range of expansion..|.....4...ins.

Complexion.......Fair

Eyes...........Blue

Hair...........Fair (yellow)

Wt. 136
lbs.

Religious denominations {
Church of England...................
Presbyterian....Yes...............
Methodist........................
Baptist or Congregationalist...........
Roman Catholic....................
Jewish...........................
Other Denominations.................
<small>(Denomination to be stated)</small>

Scar for removal of
Cervical Glands, left
side.

CERTIFICATE OF MEDICAL EXAMINATION.

I have examined the above-named Recruit and find that he does not present any of the causes of rejection specified in the Regulations for Army Medical Services.

He can see at the required distance with either eye; his heart and lungs are healthy; he has the free use of his joints and limbs, and declares that he is not subject to fits of any description.

I consider him*...*Fit........for the **Canadian Over-Seas Expeditionary Force.**

Date...Jan. 4th......1916.   R. My. F. _____

Place...Kingston Ont....   Lieut. C. M. C.
<small>* Insert here "fit" or "unfit."</small>   **Medical Officer.**

<small>Note.—Should the Medical Officer consider the Recruit unfit, he will fill in the foregoing Certificate only in the case of those who have been attested, and will briefly state below the nature of unfitness:—</small>

....

....

....

....

....

CERTIFICATE OF OFFICER COMMANDING UNIT.

Roderick Ward Maclennan having been finally approved and inspected by me this day, and his Name, Age, Date of Attestation, and every prescribed particular having been recorded, I certify that I am satisfied with the correctness of this Attestation.

Wm Begg ......(Signature of Officer)

Date......12 Feb......191 6.

He remained at this work until February 1917.

In March 1917, Ward wrote home:

"What I am about to tell you may come as a
bit of a surprise but I know you will, on
thinking the matter over, approve of it.
Just on the eve of my departure for France I
was taken of the Queen's Hospital draft and
held here, on account of an application sent
forward in February to the War Office to
secure my appointment to a commission in the
Royal Flying Corps. It appears now that I
shall be accepted and shall commence a
period of instruction. One reason for my
taking this step is because fit men are in
such great demand for fighting units.
Nothing has made me happier for a long time
than my two interviews in London with
officers at the War Office."

Further letters reveal his story...

Officers' Training School in Oxford

I have already had leisure in which to stroll about to see the architectural beauties of the town. It is undoubtedly the finest place so far as buildings go that I have seen. Beautiful vistas abound.

Go almost where you will a curving street fades into the distance, and the spot at which the curve begins is usually surmounted by some lovely tower. The effect is resting and pleasing. How I wish my family could see what I am seeing just now of old England.

One thing I have enjoyed to an enormous degree, it has taken me out of Khaki for a few hours for the first time in 16 months, is lolling about in white flannels on the river and at Christ Church tennis courts. I have had a few sets and beginning to get into fairly decent form again and to get back my old service. We are encouraged to take part in athletics all we can so I am going to try some rowing in fours. It was on the fine Saturdays and Sundays that we investigated the charms of the Isis and Cherwell and found them very good. I have had my first experience in rowing a shell with sliding seats on the Thames. It was great sport and took place on a hot June day, I was rather hoping that we would upset in transit, but we got along fairly well and managed to stay in the boat. I brought away a few blisters to remind me of the trip.

Brasenose College, Oxford, Sunday,
1st July 1917

The great thing this week is examinations, and
if we are successful, our Commission. The extra
amount of cramming that has been going or the
last few days reminds me of Osgoode Hall and
Queen's. One of the most important subjects we
have is rigging and extra stress has been laid
on it, so I have been doing a lot of scrambling
in and out of planes and through wires and I
flatter myself that rigging is one of my best
subjects. I wish I could say the same about
engines.

We have four different types to learn and
they are pretty complicated affairs you may be
sure. We had four hours of practical work on
them, running them and starting them by turning
the propeller. This is usually done by a
mechanic but an officer has to learn how it is
done, in case he has to make a forced landing
and then has to restart his engine to get home.

Photography is another branch of work taken
up but it is not very difficult. Some beautiful
instruments are used with exceptionally fine
lenses; they all work at about f/4.3. The
cameras are fixed focus and we use 4 x 5 plates
of a special kind. At the school are hundreds
of interesting aerial photographs, which are
used in conjunction with lectures. I am not
giving away any great secrets in saying that
probably every inch of the British front in
France is photographed daily.

The examinations lasted two whole days and were
held in the Corn Exchange on George Street. Many
of us were rather surprised and rather annoyed
at the simple questions asked; only about three
per cent of the applicants failed. The papers
were (1) Rotary Engines, (2) Stationary Engines,
(3) Bombs, Instruments, Photography, Wireless,
etc., (4) Rigging and Theory of Flight, (5)
Aerial Observation, and (6) A practical test in
reading Morse on the buzzer.

The examinations terminated on July 5th and
the results came out that afternoon, and my
commission dated from midnight of the 5th. On
the 6th I was sent with about 40 others to this
camp, where we shall learn to fly.

Our journey from Oxford was via Basingstoke,
where there is a Canadian hospital. We had an
hour's wait but did not see anything of the
town; being officers we travelled first class.
We then passed into the Salisbury Plain
district, which is now overrun with Australian
and New Zealand troops. We reached Bulford
about 7.45 p.m. and waited two hours until a
lorry came from the Aerodrome. Bulford was the
centre of the Canadian camp in the early days
of the war. It is a long way from anywhere and
our camp is a long way from even Bulford. We
arrived at the Aerodrome about 10 p.m. and I
found three Canadians in the Squadron to which

13

I was posted. I was assigned quarters, found my
servant, had my camp bed unpacked and turned in.

I think we are going to be comfortable here
though it is not such a civilized place as
Oxford. The Officer's Mess is near the village
on a height above the river. We have to wait on
ourselves in cafeteria style, and cannot sit
and be looked after as at Oxford. The quarters
are crowded at present and many of the new
arrivals had to go into tents. I share a room
with two others in one of the four rooms in
little white and black bungalows built of
beaver board. They have red (imitation tile)
roofs and yellow chimney pots. The Mess
resembles a good country club and has a capital
billiard room and well furnished anteroom and
in front two tennis courts. The aeroplane
sheds, half a mile east, are huge affairs,
built corrugated iron. Each flight has its own
shed. There are three squadrons with three
flights each.

The Training Camp,
8th July 1917

My first flight took place this morning, and
ended only a few minutes ago. It was in a
Maurice Farman[2] dual control machine. The
engines and propeller are behind both pupil and
pilot and so the machine is a pusher and the
pupil, who sits away out in front, has a
splendid outlook with nothing in his way. The
first fight in RFC parlance is a "Joy ride,"
and is a trip as passenger to see whether you
are going to be sick or frightened. I was
neither the one nor the other, and enjoyed
every minute in the air. We were up 15 minutes,
more or less. I was told not to watch the
ground as we were leaving it, and so I kept my
eyes on the horizon for a minute or two. Then I
took a look at the ground below and as it
seemed to be quite natural to be leaving it, I
kept on watching it getting farther and farther
away. You know how a bicycle in turning a
corner has to lean slightly in to keep from
falling outwards. An aeroplane does the same
thing in turning and this "banking" as it is
called, was hard to get used to. However when I
remembered how needlessly people are scared by
a sail boat leaning over in a still breeze, I
liked banking and hoped the pilot would do some
more, and when he did it again I hardly felt it.

The first machines used for instruction were
designed by Farman as a suitable bus in which
to fly with his wife. They are for comfort and
not speed, have 70 to 80 H.P. air cooled 8

cylinder motors and 60 miles per hour is about
the best they will do. They are slow climbers
and we only went up 600 feet. The German
attacks on London were carried out at an
altitude of 18,000 (over three miles). The
aerodrome and hangars looked very small, even
from 600 feet, and sheep in a field like pieces
of dirty rice. The first motion of the volplane
back to earth rather took my breath away but I
soon got accustomed to it. The machine had no
windscreen and as I was not wearing goggles the
speed of 60 miles rather hurt my eyes.

Prior to leaving Oxford, all who had passed their examinations visited the Quartermaster at Christ Church and were issued a flying kit, the value of which is from $150 to $200. It forms quite an imposing array and consists of a yellow leather coat to one's boot tops, with a high collar and lined with fleece wool; a yellow leather flying cap covering head, face and neck, except eyes and nose (the inside is lovely and soft, and lined with sealskin), a learner's helmet made of leather and padded with rubber and never used; sealskin gauntlets to the elbows; leather thigh boots lined with sheepskin and with red rubber soles, a large pair of rubber overshoes with cloth tops, the latter to be worn over the sheepskin high boots to keep them dry before a flight. None of these wonderful things are worn in the summer, but the coat makes an excellent bathrobe and a fine extra blanket on cold nights. We also received a camp kit which cost us about $40 folding bed, pillow, rubber sheet, bath and wash stand and a folding chair.

Being an officer now, I no longer have to clean my boots or belt. My batman is a youngish large chap of extreme deafness and as far as I can make out far from lofty intelligence. Most batmen are like this. However if he succeeds in getting me out of bed each morning at 4 a.m., in time for early flying, he will be doing something to help along the war.

The Training Camp,
15 July 1917

My second flight took place the evening
following the day of the first, and in the same
machine. It was also a "Joy ride", but this
time we climbed to 3000 feet, and came down in
a spiral of rather small radius. It was very
thrilling, and was done I think in order to
test my nerves. We came down very quickly, and
the sudden change from low to high pressure
made me quite deaf for a few minutes after
landing.

During the past week I have done three and
one half hours actual flying and I am enjoying
it very much indeed. I can not help feeling
that it would be great fun to fly around over
the islands in Lake Joseph. Flying over cities
does not appeal to me much. Out here we are far
from the habitation of man, and but for the
hutted military camps, there are no houses in
sight.

My instructor still accompanies me in the
machine but I do most of the flying and am
gaining confidence every day. Landing is
considered the most difficult thing for a
beginner but I do not find it hard and I enjoy
it. It is done in this manner: - you pick a
nice green field where the grass is fairly
short. I usually land from 200 feet; at that
height a field with short grass is easily
distinguishable. The nose of the machine is
pointed towards the earth, the engine is
throttled down to a slow speed and the machine

begins to descend. She comes pretty fast but
you hardly realize this, and are only conscious
of a steady throbbing noise as the air beats
against the planes. There is no sensation of
falling, merely gliding towards the ground.
When 12 feet off the ground you slowly pull
back your control lever (joy stick) and the
machine flattens out and runs over the grass
with little jarring or bouncing. A poorly made
landing makes the machine jump up and down and
bounce like a rubber ball. If by mistake the
pilot flattens out too soon i.e. about 20 feet
from the ground it immediately loses its
forward speed and drops like a plummet. Landing
on its wheels it usually bounds into the air,
pauses a moment, drops again, and this time
having no forward speed at all the full weight
of the machine, pilot, engine, etc., dropping
from a slight height causes the undercarriage
to break or possibly something worse happens.

Sometimes we fly over country hamlets and it
is interesting to look down at the upturned
faces of the yokels. A flock of sheep moving
across a meadow resembles, from 400 feet, a
mass of white maggots crawling, a rather nasty
description, but so it seems to me. The other
morning we passed over one of the Australian
camps just before breakfast, the men were being
given physical jerks in the barrack square,
surrounded by wooden huts. While we watched,
they began to play leap frog, and it was an
amusing spectacle. It is interesting from a
height to watch other aeroplanes sliding along
far below, giving the impression of flat white
fish swimming at a lower level in the sea. One

thing has struck me forcibly is that there is little or no noise to bother you. From the ground the machines seem to kick up a fearful row in the air. When flying you hear the engine and propeller, but it is by no means deafening, and you can easily talk to your passenger.

Machines always land into the wind so a large T is kept on the ground near the hangars, the cross piece facing the wind. This is moved when the wind changes and you know that if you land up the long part into the cross you are all right.

Our daily programme: Flying from 4.30 to 8.00 a.m. We get an hour, taking it in turn. Machine gun and wire from 10 to 11.30 a.m. Then we are usually free till from 7 to 10 p.m., when more flying is done. We spend part of the making up the sleep we lose in getting up so early. In the morning and in the evening air currents are very little disturbed by the heat of the sun.

From what I could see at Oxford certain classes are still on in all the colleges, All Souls seems entirely devoted to undergraduates. The Ladies' College "Somerville" is carrying on its usual work. In the other colleges, the students are nearly all Medicals completing their course before enlisting, or Hindus, Japanese and Americans, the latter Rhodes' scholars. Except the colleges mentioned, all others house cadets. There must be between two and three thousand there all the time. There are two infantry cadet battalions as well as the Royal Flying School of Military Aeronautics.

The Training Camp,
22 July 1917

It is Sunday morning and, wonder of wonders the
authorities have decided that for this week it
shall be a holiday.

I have now completed my instruction with
'dual control' and the night before last I was
allowed to go up alone for a short time. It was
a quiet evening and I got on quite well and the
flight increased my self confidence to a great
extent. I was a bit nervous at first but made
my landing fairly well. I did not go higher
than 500 feet. The next morning I had two
flights of half an hour each, getting in
several landings. The wind was strong and the
air bumpy, and as the wind blew over the sheds
it made taking off difficult. I scared the
Major by taking off over the sheds, instead of
through the gaps between them and I got "bawled
out" by him for this when I came down.

I am now a "soloist" as far as present
machines go, and am consequently treated with a
certain amount of respect by the other chaps
who are still going up with their instructors.
I was surprised to learn that I was the first
of the 40 who came from Oxford a fortnight ago
to do a solo flight. The instructors have
trying times in getting the chaps persuaded to
go up solo for the first time.

I have been lucky too. Landing an aeroplane
was like bringing a sailboat into a wharf. It
can be done easily by one who knows how and the
inexperienced or careless person can do it with

a bump. The undercarriage, or wheels on which
an aeroplane lands, are designed, in the
instructional machines, to break with a bump,
and thus save the more valuable parts and also
the pilot from harm. Every night someone makes
a bouncing landing, and to use a term common
here, "does in" their undercarriage. Last night
I had a crash, I bounced slightly when I
touched the ground, then lost flying speed,
"pancaked" and swerved to the left, causing my
two port wheels to turn over. I was delighted
to find that nothing was broken. The mechanics
in my flight were overjoyed when I came in
without having damaged anything at all, and I
made several landings. All the other machines
but one had breaks. This meant that the
mechanics have to spend all today fixing them.

Last Friday I spoke to one of the instructors
about Stonehenge and expressed a desire to see
it some day. He said, "Jump into my machine,
and I'll take you over before dinner". In I got
and, off we went. I had my camera and took some
photographs on the way, of the flight sheds,
our camp and of Stonehenge itself. We viewed it
first from 400ft. Stonehenge in afternoon light
makes a pretty sight from the air. The dark
green stones, each pair supporting a flat slab,
laid across them, form a large circle, set in a
light coloured green field. Quite a contrast to
the hundreds of wooden huts, part of the modern
camp nearby. We flew down quite near the
ground, as we got to the place, circled round
it for a minute, and then flew back to the
aerodrome.

Although I was the first of our bunch to do a

solo, it was not because I was rushed through.
I had careful instruction and received two
hours more dual than most get. I have got now
so that I can look about me while in the air;
at first I had looked straight ahead all the
time.

London, 26 July 1917

I completed my four hours "solo" on the
afternoon of July 23rd with great success. My
landings gradually improved as time went on and
I managed to complete my course with only one
breakage, a strut cross bracing wire, which was
repaired inside of five minutes.

I have been able to get 48 hours leave from
the camp, and so took the opportunity of
running up to town to finish getting my
clothes. I think I have everything now.

I return to the aerodrome tonight, but shall
leave it almost at once to go to a more
advanced squadron, as I have learned almost all
they can teach me at this camp.

I went last night to see a comedy called
"General Post" at the Haymarket Theatre. It
dealt with the war and was good; it has been
playing here about half a year.

Central Flying School,
28th July 1917 [3]

I am no longer at the old camp, having finished
my elementary training there. The Central
Flying School is probably the best of its kind
in England and is equipped with a fine supply
of modern machines. It is situated on a high
table land. I came here yesterday in a cloud of
dust in the tender which brought me, my luggage
and six others from the old camp.

While the old camp is fresh in my mind I
might say something of the training I received
there. I got most of my instruction from my
Squadron Commander, Major Atkinson[4]. He was a
splendid man and I believe had been with the
RFC prior to the war. A lot of confidence came
to me from his advice and "tips" and as a
result I managed to do my four hours of solo
flying with no trouble or accident of any kind.
As I was the first of my Oxford companions to
finish solo flying, this, I think, helped to
get me my two days leave, as it was almost
unheard of that leave should be granted after
completing one's elementary instruction.

Before I left the old camp, I got to
thoroughly enjoy riding around the aerodrome
alone in a "Rumpty"[5] as the instructional
machines were called. For ordinary flying
(putting in time) I used to go clackety-
clacking round at 400 feet, and soon became so
accustomed to the old busses that I could lie
back and rest and view the country and not
think much about actual flying, which became

pretty well instinctive.

The machines here are quite different; they pretty well fly themselves, and are much faster. There is not the same engine noise. The old busses used to clack away like a sewing machine or a one cylinder motor boat. Those here "hum" and would even satisfy Uncle Jim, they are so noiseless.

The Camp,
29th July 1917

As I write it is half-past three and in Muskoka
will be shortly after breakfast. I am having my
little touch of imaginary Muskoka. I had the
choice of sharing a room in a wooden hut or of
having a small bell tent pitched in a grove of
pines in rear of the Mess. I chose the tent and
am enjoying sleeping out doors again. The view
from the tent door is a wide one it overlooks
miles and miles of rolling downs.

Our Mess is a lovely place. It is a large
long one storey building built of concrete
blocks. The ceilings are high and there are
large windows everywhere. It has a big lobby,
a, huge dining room, a large billiard room, two
writing rooms, a card room and the anteroom
which is a long rectangular room with its
southern side all windows and has several sky
lights, the whole effect tending towards that
of a studio. I have several times thought of
trying some photographs there. The floor is
tiled and covered with rugs and the walls
decorated with deer's heads. The dining room is
also a big bright room and the walls are hung
with good oil paintings. The Mess as a whole is
more like a large hotel than an implement of
war. I suppose it will be kept on as a training
centre after the war.

I had rather hoped that life with the RFC
might make me grow a bit thinner, but we have
such splendid meals that I am beginning to
despair. I have never had such good food, such
variety and such tasty cooking as we are
enjoying at present. It has Oxford completely
beaten, although the surroundings are not as
impressive. The Mess is also much better and
incidentally much more expensive, than at the
old camp.

30th July 1917

Notes for the Fighting Pilot

I keep this note book for the purpose of
collecting in it every possible bit of
information I can pick up on flying and aero-
fighting and to record every incident of
interest and instructive use on every flight. I
shall be surprised how interesting and
instructive it will soon become.

The first few notes are written with the
intention of impressing upon me the importance
of making myself efficient and how effective I
can be if efficient; also to give me an ideal
which it is absolutely necessary I should work
up to. The ideal is by no means perfect, and
until I can thoroughly satisfy myself that I
have reached it, I cannot hope, to count myself
amongst the ranks of fighting pilots who count
overseas.

As a single fighting unit I have the means of
doing more damage to the enemy than any other
in the whole army.

At the Camp, 5th August 1917

It is nine a.m. and owing to numerous "bumps"
in the air and low clouds and mist, flying has
been "washed out" for this morning so I shall
be able to write letters, read and have a lazy
time. You never saw such weather. It has rained
and blown and been misty every single day for a
whole week. I have only had two flights since
coming to Upavon and they were over a week ago
and lasted only an hour altogether. It became
monotonous sitting about waiting so I applied
for leave and proceeded to Bath last Wednesday
and returned here Friday night.

The friends I visited have been there for
four years and in that time have developed an
almost unbelievable garden. It contains almost
every kind of flower and vegetable that I ever
heard of and in addition has peach, pear, cherry
and apple trees, all bearing fruit; and
strawberries, raspberries, loganberries, and
gooseberries. The loganberries are a cross
between blackberries and raspberries and they
are said to grow better than rhubarb. The
berries are large and slightly tarter than
raspberries. It almost made me laugh to think of
our efforts for years and years to get a decent
peach off our one tree, when theirs is bearing a
large crop after only three years. They did not
raise it from seed however. Besides all this,
they have about 30 chickens and eight or nine
rabbits. Their table always had their own
lettuce and salads on it and the first night I
was with them they had a fine marrow.

My batman here is a constant source of worry.

He does the ordinary things, such as boots, belt, buttons etc., pretty well but he has an insatiable habit of searching through all my belongings, especially on Mondays, in order to send my clothes to the wash Last week he sent nearly everything I own, including my winter underwear and a suit of pyjamas I had never worn. When I came here first, he unpacked all my stuff and spread it all over and about my tent, with a sort of decorative effect. I usually prefer to have my belongings, not in immediate use, packed up in my kit bag and it took him several days to see this and to learn that I did not want him to drag all my family skeletons out into public view. He is a very useful chap and I don't know what I shall do when the war is over. Even three days in Bath without him made me feel lost.

The life agrees with me and I am enjoying it. I hardly know how I shall ever be able to settle down again after the war.

Our programme at Upavon, is as follows. Early morning when detailed, breakfast at 7.30 a.m. followed by a parade at the sheds at 8.20. Flying takes place all morning weather permitting but during the forenoon an hour is spent at machine guns, an hour at artillery observation and half an hour at a lecture or drill. We have the afternoons off till 4.30 p.m. when evening flying commences, this lasts till 8.45 when we rush to the Mess and "gobble up" what remains of dinner which had been served at eight. Luncheon is at 12.45 and tea at 4 p.m. Instead of a few waiters, we have a small army of waitresses who look after us very well.

The Camp,
12th August 1917

The past week has been a dull one; continual
rain day after day has made flying and
certainly instruction impossible. Yesterday I
had a "Joy ride" in one of the very fast
machines. It was fine and gave me all sorts of
thrills. The chief disadvantage is the stream
of castor oil which the rotary engine throws
out all over the machine, pilot and passenger.
The fastest machines of all are tiny little
things and carry only one man. They have
stationary engines and are not nearly so dirty
as those I have just mentioned.

I had a letter recently from one of the chaps
at Westenhanger, and he tells me that quite a
number are joining the flying service as a
result of the step I took. On Thursday I was
inoculated for typhoid and consequently had a
sore arm for a day or two. It is all over now.
This was my first inoculation since the dose I
had in Kingston in 1916.

About first flights. The first couple were
merely joy rides during which I became
accustomed to the 'feel' of being off the
ground, turning, banking, etc. The remainder of
the five or six hours I spent on dual control.
The practice machines are fitted up with one
set of control levers, rudder bar, throttle and
switch for the instructor, and a duplicate set
of each for the pupil. The latter rests his
hands and feet lightly on the controls while
the instructor does the actual flying. Each
movement made by the instructor is felt by the
hands and feet of the pupil, who soon begins to
associate the action of the machine with the
different movements of the controls. Later on
the pupil takes control and the instructor
merely rests his hands on the levers. Still
later the pupil takes full control and the
teacher (who is behind) rests his hands on the
pupil's shoulders to show him that at last he
is actually flying the machine alone, usually
greatly to the surprise of the latter.

After this, a fine morning is chosen when
there is not much wind and the young birdman
tremblingly sets forth on his first solo
flight. He goes round the aerodrome once or
twice and then essays a landing and if he
carries this out successfully, his confidence
is increased enormously and, he usually gets on
pretty well.

This morning one of the instructors took me
for a "joy ride"' on one of the fastest

machines, an "Avro"[6]. We were bound for a nearby aerodrome, but at 3000 feet the clouds got so thick that we had to turn back. The clouds were the great white ones piled up one another against a deep blue sky on a summer day. We found ourselves in a sort of gorge, which seemed to run for miles between huge banks of the white clouds. Far below us as we looked down the lane between the clouds lay a bright green strip of fields. On either side, almost touching the wing tips of our machine was an impenetrable mass of snowy white cloud-bank. Far above us as we looked up through the canyon walls was a strip of bright blue sky. This gorge of clear air between the clouds, although very narrow, extended several miles back to the aerodrome. It was great.

The Camp,
19 August 1917

Since leaving Oxford I have had quite a little
opportunity for reading and have read all kinds
of things, some of the better books being:
Conan Doyle's "Micah Clarke" and part of
"Martin Chuzzlewit", one or two of Alexander
Dumas' tales, two humorous books by George
Birmingham about small Irish villages, and one
or two of Bernard Shaw's plays.

I am still doing dual control on B.E. 2b
machines which are quite out of date for
military purpose and were obsolete even before
the war. They are good busses for instructional
purposes for if one can fly one of these, he
can fly anything else made. Our pet name for
these antediluvian birds is "Hunguffin". The
Farman machines, on which I learned to fly, are
called "Rumpties". Nearly all machines have
similar pet names. One rather popular type of
scout machine is called a "Pup" because of its
small size. Another is called a "Camel" because
its planes have a peculiar humped appearance,
when looking at them from the front.[7] It will be
another month before I have anything to do with
either Pups or Camels, as, when I finish with
Hunguffins, I have to learn to fly Avros before
going on to the smaller scout machines.

Fog and low clouds hold us back a great deal.
Fog is the worst and then it is not safe to go
up as it is difficult to see the ground and
hard to land properly. A good lookout is kept
from the ground when the machines are up and if

34

a fog is seen approaching, white rockets are
sent up and all machines must land at once. The
rockets burst high up, above the clouds if they
are low ones, and the flashes are easily seen.
This happened once in my early experience.

During the past week I had several rides in
an Avro. Probably the most thrilling thing you
can do with an Avro is "stalling". This is a
safety arrangement to enable a machine get into
a proper gliding position in case of engine
failure. First, when flying level you get up a
good speed, then gradually point the machine's
nose up and up until she climbs so steeply that
the engine will take her no further. Then, if
the engine is shut off, the machine will tail
slide a short distance, then her nose will drop
and she will dive and from this she is
gradually flattened out again. The dive is a
fine thrilling sensation and has tobogganing

B.E.2.C.

beaten a long way. The machine is so designed
that she will come out of the dive herself,
although the pilot usually pulls her out.

The controls of all these machines are
simple. The main one is the "joy stick", a
handle which comes up from the floor between
the pilot's feet. To go up, the stick is pulled
towards the pilot, to go down, it is pushed
forward and the engine shut off. To turn to the
left the stick is moved towards the left and
this tilts the planes to the left, at the same
time the left foot, which is resting on the
rudder bar, in front of the joy stick, is
pushed slightly forward, this with the left
bank which you have previously put on the
machine turns her to the left. When the turn is
made you press gently on the rudder bar with
the right foot to make it central again, at the
same time you take off the bank by moving the
joy stick slightly to the right. The whole
thing soon becomes instinctive, and you do it
all without thinking about it.

I have been exploring the country by road on
a rented bicycle, and it has been very
pleasant. Our one great drawback is
remoteness. The School is miles from the
nearest railway and the same distance from
even a small town. One afternoon I went nearly
to Devizes on a bicycle. I expect to go all
the way next time. There is a beautiful road
and no bad hills. I passed quite close to the
white horse cut out of chalk on the hill side.[8]
As soon as I start solo I shall fly over it
and take an aerial photograph.

When we are detailed for early morning

36

flying we do not worry about waking up at 5
a.m. in time to get to the sheds at 5.30. Part
of the duties of the air mechanics, privates in
the RFC and technically known as "Ack Emmas,"
is to wake us in time for flying. In case the
weather is not suitable we are not wakened at
all. When we are wakened we have to sign a slip
of paper to the effect that we were called.
This the Ack Emma retains in case we should go
off to sleep again.

London, 25th August 1917

I persuaded the authorities to let me have a
couple of days leave this weekend.

It is amusing to see the Sammie's[9] about the
London streets. They cannot help looking,
acting and feeling new. It is great fun taking
and returning their salutes, and while they
look a fine body of men, I shall be very
surprised if they do not earn a worse name for
discipline than our own Canadians.

I have just come into the hotel after walking
up the Strand from Trafalgar Square, and there
were crowds of these chaps on the streets. It
has not taken the London street girls long to
find them out and as the Sammies are pretty
well paid, they are bound to receive all kinds
of attention from these ladies.

At the Camp,
28th August 1917

I got back to the School just ahead of a storm,
which made Sunday night blustery. I thought the
tent would go before morning. It cleared about
5 a.m. on Monday, and I was able to get a short
flight before breakfast. Soon afterwards rain
clouds appeared again and ever since we have
live in a deluge. I was wet through for the
first time since I left the Military Hospital
and till after lunch, when I got a chance to
change, I was rather uncomfortable. The rest of
the afternoon I dozed on my bed covered up by
my leather coat and listened to the rain
beating on the tent roof.

Owing to the bad weather, which has prevailed
ever since I came to the Central School, I am
still on dual control. I am now ready for solo
and wait for a decent day on which to begin.
They are careful here to choose good weather to
start beginners on their first flights alone.

If I should be unlucky enough to break one or
two machines in landing, I will be sent to an
Artillery Training Squad for further
instruction. This is the fate that befalls a
great many, some of whom have been here for a
long time. However, in nearly two months
flying, I have not broken anything yet and am
not likely to do so now.

The Camp,
2nd September 1917

Until today, the wet stormy weather continued
and consequently I am still on dual controls
and am getting an excellent chance to learn
everything.

The first serious accident occurred a few
days ago. Most accidents occur on the type of
elementary machines I flew at the beginning.
They are the hardest of any to fly, and I am
glad I am successfully finished with them. The
smash occurred to a chap named Wood from
Kingston. I went to college with him and I
believe his father is a missionary in India.
His machine nosedived about 200 feet to the
ground and there was not enough of it left to
think of repairing it. Every bit was smashed to
atoms and yet Wood was practically unhurt. He
had a black eye, a scratch on his head and a
tooth knocked out and nothing else. I went to
see him in the hospital yesterday and he
expects to be flying again in almost no time.
Only one bad smash in about 3000 flights, since
I have been here, and that one only slightly
shaken up, looks pretty safe, does it not?

This afternoon I spent playing singles on our
lovely tennis courts. You never would think
there was a war going on to look at Upavon this
afternoon. Motor parties leaving and arriving
at the Mess, tennis players in white flannels,
golfing enthusiasts, male and female, dotted
all over the links which stretch away in front
of the Mess, and an occasional aeroplane

humming and whining overhead. Sunday afternoon
flying is voluntary and not many machines are
about. If you had strolled through the camp on
the opposite side from the Mess, the sight of a
barbed wire enclosure, guarded by sentries,
would have disillusioned you. These chaps are
kept here to be employed on heavy manual
labour, such as digging septic tanks, making
roads etc. They are a contented lot and seem to
work pretty well.

I have made my first solo flight at the Central
Flying School. I managed it all right, making
several good landings and was complimented by
my instructor. It was made in a B.E 2b, an
almost pre-war type of machine, which is hard
to fly, especially in bumps. I have now done
six hours on this machine and in a few days
will go on to Avros which are steadier and
easier to fly.

A couple of days last week I was not quite up
to the mark and was not allowed to fly at all.
That is one of the things they watch carefully
in the Central Flying School. No one is allowed
to take a machine in the air unless in the pink
of condition. All I had was a slight cold which
gave me a stiff neck for a day or two.

A meagre description of afternoon flying. We
have to be at the sheds at 4.10 p.m. In front,
of them runs a strip of tarred road surface 50
feet wide. On this the machines stand while
waiting to go up; it is called the "Tarmac". We
have a roll call at 4.15 p.m., and then sit in
the sun on the tarmac with our "funny hat" and
goggles. Presently a loud spluttering and then
a deep hum from one of the 40 machines lined
up, is the signal for the commencement of the
evening work. One of the instructors is going
up to test the air. Up he goes, does a couple
of circuits round the aerodrome, lands, and
says: "2b pupils can wash out till six o'clock.
Avros had better stay." This means that it is

too bumpy for B.E. 2b's but safe for Avros.
Being a 2b artist, I go back to the Mess or to
my tent to read for an hour or so, and by the
time I get there a dozen machines are in the
air and the throbbing hum of their engines is
pretty loud. By the time I get well into my
book the sound is no longer heard, although it
is still there. One becomes unconscious of the
racket, especially in the early morning, when
ones lucky enough not to be on early flying and
can sleep peacefully through a row that would
put an army of steel automatic riveting
machines to shame.

I go back to the shed at six and the air
above the camp is thick with machines. In one
place two Camels and a Pup are practicing aerial
fighting and are chasing each other up and down
and around with all kinds of weird engine
noises. Farther over and very high up five Avros
are practising "formation flying"; keeping close
together they are following their leader who has
a long streamer flying from his rudder. From the
ground they, resemble a small flock of birds,
and they are so high that their engines cannot
be heard above the hum of those below.

Quite near the ground a few pupils are
practising under watchful eyes of their
instructors, whose flow of language is
surprisingly copious, should the landing prove
a specially bad one.

Half a mile away, out in the centre of the
aerodrome, a pilot is practicing in his
machine. He has been careless in landing and
has "lost his prop!" In other words he has
stalled his engine and has to sit there till a

mechanic can run out to start him up again.
Needless to say, pupils who do this sort of
thing frequently are most unpopular with the
mechanics. Swinging a propeller is no easy task
but when it entails a half mile walk at each
end of the job, it is rather worse.

Over by the sheds a number of pupils are
waiting their turn to go up. One of them in a
machine is nervously running his engine
preparatory to going up alone for the first
time. His instructor is standing on the side of
the machine watching the instruments and
shouting directions. The engine is slowed down
and off goes the machine, first slowly over the
grass till it reaches the centre of the
aerodrome, then with roaring engine, and
heading into the wind, it tears along the
ground, rises and floats up and up till it
becomes a speck five miles away. From this
moment until 15 minutes later when the machine
again approaches the sheds, and prepares to
land, is a trying time for the instructor who
can do nothing but look on. This pupil makes a
fair landing and, proud as punch, gets out of
his machine and is told that he can "wash out"
for the remainder of the evening.

I have been detailed to do a reconnaissance
of two roads, each about 10miles long, with a
view to their suitability for concealment of
infantry from aircraft, facilities for watering
horses, condition and traffic. In addition I
have been shown two spots on the map and have
been told to ascertain what is on the ground at
these points.

I get in my machine, put on my leather cap

and tie a pencil on the end of a string to my
belt. Then I fold my map so that the spot I
have to cover is visible and then strap my map
to my left leg above the knee with one of my
garters. I do the same with a notebook on my
right knee and after a final polish of my
goggles I am ready. The next three minutes is
spent in testing the engine. This is found to
be O.K. I wave my arm, do up my belt, the
chocks are taken away from beneath my wheels
and I slowly taxi out, looking for other
machines, then heading to wind I take off.

Up comes the tail, and over the ground I go
for about 200 yards. When a speed of 50 miles
an hour is reached the machine takes herself
off the ground and starts to climb. When 1000
feet is reached I slow down slightly and fly
level. Presently I reach one of the spots to be
examined. It is between a road and a wood and
appears to be nothing more than green grass.
Nothing is unusual so the engine is shut off
and down she goes to 400 feet for a closer
look. From this height I can just make out a
newly dug hole about four feet in diameter and
near it two more. I mark these on the map, make
a note of their size and fly off in the
direction of the other spot. To reach it I have
to pass over a large wood and then some
ploughed fields and expecting bumps from these,
I climb to 1000 feet, before passing over them.
But even then I feel them and the old bus jumps
around as if she were alive. The spot brings me
over a farm. Again I come down to 400 feet and
in the centre of the lawn in front of the farm
house are two white strips. A "T" is quite

plain and something resembling "H" was beside it. Hurried notes are made of these strips, and the machine is headed for where the road reconnaissance is to begin. I have been told to do it from 4000 feet, but at 2000 I am getting into the clouds and as the bumps from them are pretty bad, I come down to 1500 and do the scheme from there. The two roads, 16 miles, are done in 15 minutes, hasty notes being made as I go. One of them I find much more suitable for the required purpose than the other, on account of woods and trees through which it runs. It also winds alongside the river, and consequently would be good for watering purposes.

At this stage, just as I am admiring the sunset, which is a gorgeous one, and am thinking it time to return to the aerodrome, my engine begins to splutter and gives signs of "conking out". This is because I have been up an hour and a half and have used up all the petrol in my top tank. So I begin pumping the supply from the reserve tank into the top one and the engine, now quite satisfied, picks up and runs merrily again. There are few machines up now, as it is almost dinner time. It is beginning to get dark and as I am gliding down an occasional jet of flame from my exhaust can be seen. It gives a weird effect, especially from the ground.

Soon the grass is tearing along right under me. I feel the wheels running along it, and the next minute I am undoing my belt and getting rid of my map, notebook and goggles. The machine is left to the care of the mechanics, and I am off to the Mess to eat a huge dinner and then to roll into bed.

London,
15th September 1917

I managed to get some leave and have been in
London for the past two days. I have seen some
of the damage done by German bombs.[10] They make
great holes in the street and break all the
glass for many hundred feet.

Getting out of Clapham Common after the
theatre was quite a problem. All the theatres
seem to empty about the same time and the tubes
were simply jammed. I have been in some pretty
thick London crowds on previous occasions, but
never with a girl to look after and we had
rather a time to keep together. It was managed
all right, but I had enough of the underground
for one night, and came back to Westminster on
the upper deck of an electrical tram by which
hangs a tale. I have crossed the Atlantic Ocean
without a qualm, I have been present at post
mortems which would sicken a stone image, I
have negotiated the upper air in bumpy weather
with confidence and buoyancy but I was almost
sick to my disgust. I did not actually "throw
up" but I was never nearer it since that
memorable occasion on the Corona when returning
from Le Roy 12 years ago or more. London trams
are very slow and the one I was in had the
upper deck roofed over and enclosed. The
beastly things roll a lot and generally are
creations of the devil.

The following day I spent doing a little
shopping, visiting my tailor, book stores, etc.
I called at Burberry's and had a fleece lining

fitted to my trench coat. I also purchased a
pair of heavy leather gauntlets for use in the
machine both for warmth and to keep my hands
clean. I visited the best barber I could find
as the CFS artist who made two attempts at
cutting my hair, made a frightful mess of it
each time. All this and a trip to Cox & Co., my
bankers, took most of the day.

Central Flying School,
19th September 1917

We are fortunate at this school, which is one
of the largest and best in England. It is an
honour to have been chosen for it. Here, Scout
pilots are trained and having been the original
scout squadron prior to the war, it has a
reputation to maintain.

Although remarkably free from serious
accidents, we do smash up a good many machines.
In order to cope with this it is almost a small
industrial community as well as a flying
school. The repair and assembling sheds and the
engine shops would shame the average Canadian
manufacturing town. About 100 machines are kept
in flying condition and about a quarter as many
are in dry dock.

The Mess is first class and the facilities
for recreation and activities rival a good
country club. We have squash courts, football
and baseball fields, excellent golf links, and
tennis courts that equal those of the best club
in Toronto. The man power problem is acute over
here and every position that can be filled by
women is so filled. All the cooks, waiters,
clerks, etc. are girls, and all the mechanical
transport vehicles, except the heaviest
lorries, are also driven by girls. Having so
many women in the lines would seem to create
rather a problem for those in charge of
discipline but it works out remarkably well.
There has been no trouble so far and various
social events have been arranged with success.

About the middle of August we held a sports day, followed in the evening by a large dance. This was well patronized, not only by the officers but by the other ranks too. It seems almost incredible that in a British Military Unit such a thing could happen.

At the Central Flying School,
23rd September 1917

I have just begun solo on Avros, having done
about 15 hours very successful flying on
Hunguffins without smashing a single thing.
Rather a record I think. I am very pleased in
consequence. Avros are quite different to fly.
They are stable in the air, practically fly
themselves, and if they get into a nasty
position, come out of it themselves. The other
busses I have been on will not do this and are
not so safe; I am glad I am through with them.

    I got lost this morning for the first time.
Five machines went up together to fly in
formation. I was the second on the right. After
we had been up for a while we all got into a
cloud and, as a precaution against getting too
close to the rest, I put my nose down and came
out of it. I could not find the others
anywhere, and we were miles away from the
aerodrome. I did not recognise any of the
surrounding countryside. If I had not had my
compass, I should have had to land and ask
where I was, as I had no map with me. By
steering south I came to a town I recognised.
This relieved me very much. I knew the way from
there and in 20 minutes regained the "drome". I
was glad I did not have to land, as it makes
one feel foolish to ask where you are, and have
some yokel volunteer the information that you
are in Master Brown's field. When I got back to
the aerodrome it was just in time to catch up
with the rest of the flight and we all landed

together in perfect formation. I enjoyed this
morning's flip, as in formation all one does is
to keep one's eyes on the leader and do just as
he does. If one gets engine trouble, one has to
drop out, but that does not happen often.

During the week 15 American soldiers arrived
here to, be trained as Ack Emmas (air
mechanics).Tonight we had two American officers
in the Mess.

This afternoon I went to the village to call
at the Alexander's. At one time they were the
family of this part of Wiltshire and owned most
of the land about there. Mrs. A. asked me to
walk to Rushall" with her to visit her
husband's mother, who lived in a real country
house. As I seemed interested in English
Country places they showed me all over the
house. It was a charming place, large and
rambling. The dining room was panelled in oak,
and the kitchens, pantries and sculleries
seemed endless. The bedrooms were old fashioned
and each had a huge four-poster. Of course the
roof was thatched. The garden was fine, and
from the house the view through the garden and
over the distant downs, was lovely. I had a
pleasant afternoon.

Last night we had a nice time in the Mess.
The orchestra played for an hour after the
meal, and then we had an impromptu concert. I
have got very attached to the Mess. Four of us
go about together and have a happy time. I get
homesick for them and it, when I go on leave,
and am always glad to get back.

Accidents here are not common, unfortunately
they seem much too common at home. No stunts

are allowed in any spirit of bravado. I think I
shall be here another month. Then I shall be
fully trained and shall in all probability
cross to France. I must close now as it, is
getting late and I am in a formation for early
tomorrow morning. I am still in tents.

Central Flying School,
26th September 1917

On Monday morning I first flew an hour's
formation with five other "Hunguffins". Then I
was sent up to do an hour in an Avro. When I
came down I got orders to go as a passenger to
Farnborough near Aldershot. The Captain who
flew the machine was to bring back a scout
machine to the school and I was to fly back the
Hunguffin. My Squadron Commander knew that I
wanted to spend a night in Oxford, so he told
me, just as I went off, that if I happened to
get lost on the way back and found Oxford,
nothing would be said about it.

We left the School at one o'clock and were at
Farnborough, 50 miles away, in an hour. We had
lunch and as soon as I could get my machine
filled up with petrol and oil, I started out.
The weather was perfect. I followed the railway
to Basingstoke, then north to Reading and the
Thames from there to Oxford. Helped by a good
wind I seemed to get there in no time, taking
less than an hour. Between Reading and Oxford I
got lost for a few minutes, eventually finding
myself over Wallingford, which I at first
thought was Oxford. There was no mistaking
Oxford however, once seen. Christ Church and
the Radcliffe Camera are splendid landmarks.
The City is a beautiful sight from 3000 feet,
and the aerodrome at Port Meadow, a huge one,
can be seen from miles away.

I headed straight for the aerodrome, made a
fairly good landing about four o'clock and

obtained permission from the adjutant, whom I knew, to have my machine looked after for the night. Then I jumped into a side-car which was going into town, and in 10minutes was at the house of Mr and Mrs Gerran's of Worcester College having tea. They all made quite a fuss over their first visitor in an aeroplane. I was rather tired from the trip and was glad to get to bed early. Unfortunately I had missed Ted Mackay who had been with them the previous day.

I left early the following morning but when I went out to the aerodrome the weather was so threatening that the Commanding Officer would not let me start back. By three o'clock it improved slightly although it was misty. The clouds were at 2000 feet and as they were too thick to see through if I had gone above them, I had to fly just below them at 1500 feet, so I was bumped about pretty badly. I found my way all right and reached Netheravon about four, doing 60 miles in just sixty minutes. I had tea there, got more oil and petrol, and in 10 minutes after leaving I was back safe and sound at the school, where I was 'strafed' by my Squadron commander for having stayed to tea at Netheravon.

On a clear day one can see a town 30 miles away but yesterday was so cloudy and misty that I had to come down to 1000 feet to see objects directly below me. Cross country flying on a clear day is delightful, but in "dud" weather it is not pleasant.

Central Flying School,
29th September 1917

On my return to the school late Tuesday
afternoon, I flew again till dark and also on
the following day until noon when I went into
Devizes to see the dentist. I was advised to
have a wisdom tooth extracted. Part was removed
and as a result I have been nursing a sore jaw
and a swollen face and have not been allowed to
fly since. It is now Sunday and I have just got
permission to have a short trip this morning.

When I made my memorable flight to Oxford I
found I was the first guest Mrs Gerrans had
ever had by air. As a result I was bombarded by
questions, and the most amusing part of the
visit was the attitude of the two maids in the
house. They had seen me before and knew who I
was and they were also expecting me as I had
telephoned the previous evening. All during
dinner the maid who was waiting on the table
kept looking at me with eyes as big as saucers.
On this trip I burned about 30 gallons of
petrol and 10 pints of oil.

I have now finished with D Squadron and am
being sent to C. My quarters and Mess remain
the same. I will go on flying Avros for the
present as I have not done much time on them.
When I said good-bye to my late Squadron
Commander he was very nice and said that any
time I wanted a machine on a Sunday or at slack
times during the week, he thought he could
spare me a Hunguffin. This may come in useful
some time and I shall not forget it. Speaking

of these machines, some nonsense about them in
limerick form, written one day when I had
nothing better to do. "Guffin" is the pet name
for the B.E. 2b.

A certain sky pilot said "Why
Can't I fly upside down if I try?"
But his bus, a 2B,
Tipped him into the sea,
Saved his life, but he couldn't keep dry.

Another young chap said "I must
Loop the loop with my "guffin", or bust",
When he'd finished his stunt
His tail was in front
And his wing tips were wound round his
thrust.

Moral —

If you wish to aviate a "2B",
Don't be hasty just listen to me.
Stick around the ground,
It's much safer, I've found,
If you must attain height, climb a tree.

Yesterday and today have been almost summer
days with just a touch of crispness in the air.
I have moved my camp chair and table outside my
tent, and sitting there under the pine trees I
am spending an hour or so writing.
As I write, Hetherington, one of our
particular four is buzzing through the sky at a
great height on an S.E.5 machine, trying to
take photographs at close range of another

56

scout of the same kind. They are having a great
time dodging and chasing each other. Just now
they have passed out of sight but they will be
over again in a moment or so as they can fly
120 miles an hour.

At the Central Flying School,
6th October 1917

I am detailed for duty tomorrow as Squadron
Orderly Officer and I shall be fairly busy
all day.

Yesterday our canvas camp in the pretty pine
grove was struck and now I am sharing a small
panelled room in a wooden hut with Lieutenant
Hemsworth, an Irish boy who is one of our four.

Since I came to C Squadron a week ago I have
done very little flying. I have been in the air
less than three hours. This has been mainly due
to the wet windy weather and partly to the fact
that the Squadron is overcrowded at present so
having done an hour's flying, each chap is
"washed out" for the remainder of the day in
order to allow the others a chance to use the
buses. I made a special effort to get
transferred to C because I like the machine
from which C men graduate. It is a tiny one
with a stationary engine and can fly level at
120 miles an hour and dive at 200. I am still
on Avros, not being ready yet for this new
buss.

This morning I was cold in the air for the
first time. I went up before breakfast, and did
an hour buzzing in and out among the clouds; to
get clear of them I had to go up to 5000 feet,
nearly a mile, and although it was all blue and
gold up there, with snowy white in a great
saucer below me, yet it was bitterly cold. When
I came down I dived through gaps in the clouds
when I could find them, as it is unsafe to fly

straight through thick clouds for fear of
collision. I got down in time to get a couple
of eggs some bacon, toast and coffee. They
tasted fine and soon warmed me up again. I did
not fly again today and with the exception of
an hour at machine guns I had the rest of the
day to myself.

I have been enjoying the change from B.E.2B
machines to Avros. After 15 hours on the former
I got very confident in them, yet they have not
the steadiness and power which an Avro
possesses. The latter has a 100 horse power
rotary engine; and it is great fun taking off.
The machine rolls over the ground faster and
faster, your instrument shows her going 20,
then 30, 40 and 50 miles an hour. About this
point she leaves the ground. You do not feel
her rising much and are never conscious of the
exact minute the wheels leave the earth. But as
soon as you do, the speed suddenly jumps to 60
or 70 miles an hour. Even at this speed she is
climbing and when you shove her nose down so
that she is flying level she will do 80 miles
an hour quite easily. The pilot is not
conscious of these speeds. The speed indicator,
mounted on the instrument board in front of his
knees, alone lets him know the difference
between 40 and 80 miles. This along with the
"rev" counter, which shows how fast the engine
is revolving and the altimeter, a barometer
which shows the height in 1000's of feet, are
the three chief instruments found on every
aeroplane. An Avro will climb to a height equal
to the City Hall tower at home in less than two
minutes from the time it commences running over

the ground taking off.

I have spoken of the disagreeable bumps in the air near the ground and in the vicinity of clouds. This machine is so well designed that bumps need hardly be considered by the pilot. They chuck his machine about and would do this to any bus made but an Avro corrects these herself and the pilot does not have to be continually waggling the stick about as he does on a B.E. 2B.

When the engine is shut off and the nose of the machine pointed towards the earth in order to come down, the beginner usually has a horrible sinking feeling about the stomach. This sensation entirely disappears as one does more and more flying and now I never notice it in the slightest degree. Gliding back to earth is probably the most pleasing sensation of any. An Avro will glide down at 70 miles an hour with the engine off, without the pilot's hands touching any of the controls. During the glide the machine can be made to turn in any direction for a straight glide, or come down like a soaring bird in a spiral. The latter is a useful mode of getting into a small field from a point directly above it.

Last evening, Hemsworth[12] and I and two of our Emma Tocks (which is morse alphabet for M.T.-motor transport) went to Devizes to a dance at the Town Hall in aid of a Red Cross Fund. We left in a Ford car about half past six and got back to camp after one. The girls were two sisters who have been driving cars since I came to the school. Their evening dress and dancing were quite up to the mark and we had a

first rate time. This was the first dance I had
been at since a memorable affair in Folkestone
last February. The Town Hall made a fine
ballroom much resembling the famous Assembly
Room in Bath. (The latter by the way are now
being used for the manufacture of aeroplane
parts). Most of the men were officers from the
surrounding camps, so we did not feel much out
of water. We had a nice ride back and greatly
to my relief I was not on the early morning
flying list for the next day. Tonight I am
going to bed early and my batman has just put a
hot water bottle in my blankets. I shall finish
this some time tomorrow.

Next morning

It is still cold and raining hard. I am keeping
warm by wearing my fur lined hip boots in my
room. In half an hour I go to the sheds to see
that everything is in order and I shall have to
change into something more waterproof. I am
rather annoyed at the rain, Sunday afternoons
are usually a holiday and I shall not be able
to have the long walk and I tea at Enford[13]
which I had planned.

We do not pin much faith on the U.S.A. aero
motor which is to be standardized, and made in
large quantities. Standardisation checks
improvement and a machine is out of date,
sometimes, as quickly as three months from its
first appearance.

Central Flying School,
9th October 1917

I have developed into quite a country bird,
having hardly been in a town (with the
exception of Oxford) for nearly six months. The
summer in Wiltshire was delightful but now the
cold autumn weather is setting in, bringing
strong winds and frequent rain to such an
extent that I have only been in the air about
four hours during the last two weeks.

The School here is crowded at present and as
a result of the bad weather few are being
passed out. There are far more colonial chaps
than Englishmen and the Canadians easily lead
the lot in point of numbers.

Since my cross country flight to Oxford I
have gone on to receive instruction on faster
machines, and the change has been quite a
welcome one. There is a good deal to learn
about them, and it will be some time yet before
I feel as much at home in the new bus as I did
in the old one.

A chap "blew in" here the other day from
Toronto. He had been in the year ahead of me at
Osgoode Hall, and had received some instruction
at Camp Borden. From what I can learn the
Canadian Aviation Schools manage to kill off a
large number of their pupils in the early
stages. We are much more fortunate here and
while we have lots of crashes, there are very
few fatal ones.

The mornings and evenings are so dark now
that little flying is attempted before 7 a.m.

or after 5.30 p.m. This gives us much more
sleep than we had in the summer but we have
practically no time off during the day.

Central Flying School,
12th October 1917

I had an experience the other day. The shutter
of my camera suddenly went "dud" and as it is
impossible to have repairs done in England now,
I took the whole "blooming" thing apart, fixed
it, and after about I three hours managed to
put it together again.

The weather is seriously interfering with
flying just now. Flying in the rain is
decidedly unpleasant. At 80 miles an hour rain
drops cut into one's face like hailstones and
the accumulation of rain and oil on the goggles
makes it hard to see. This morning, I had my
goggles blow completely off in the air. I was
lucky to make a successful grab at them just as
they were disappearing overboard. I found the
lenses had been pushed out of their sockets, so
I had to land in order to effect repairs.

The Squadron in our school which does most
flying during the week gets two days off over
the weekend. Ours led by a long way last week
and if the weather is fine tomorrow I think I
shall fly again to Oxford. If it is too wet, I
shall go by train.

20 St. John Street, Oxford,
14th October 1917

I am having a clear holiday from Saturday noon
to Sunday night. I had a warm invitation to
repeat my recent visit to Mr. and Mrs. Gerrans
and I have done so. I had planned to fly to
Oxford again and having warned my hostess that
I was coming and having got my machine ready to
start, I learned that the aerodrome at Oxford
was temporarily closed and that the authorities
there could give no assistance to pilots
landing on cross country flights. I had to
change my plans and come by train. I reached
Oxford about tea time Saturday afternoon having
left the school at 11.30 a.m.

Last night I spent quietly in the house. This
morning I went with Mrs. Gerrans to the University
Service in St. Mary's Church. It was over at 11.30
a.m. and in the interval before lunch, I had a
walk about the town. We visited several of my old
haunts including Brasenose and in addition I saw
the inside of New College for the first time. We
finished by going through the University Park.

The University Service in St. Mary's this
morning would, I think, have shocked the
average Episcopalian Church goer, or at least
he would have been surprised at the form it
took. The ubiquitous Book of Common Prayer was
neither used nor followed. There was one hymn,
one prayer and a sermon which really took the
form of an argument in favour of increased
theological training for the clergy. The
congregation was not large and with the

exception of myself was comprised exclusively
of University dignitaries, their families and a
few undergraduates. It turned out the finest
day we have had in two months, so that walk
after the service was most enjoyable.

On Friday I received Mother's letter of 16th
September. Dad had added a query as to whether
'looping' was necessary. It is not, except in
very exceptional circumstances, during possibly
a very hard fight. In spite of warnings some
foolish pilots will persist in doing it in
machines which are not strong enough for this
stunt. On small, strong scout machines like a
Camel it can be done with perfect safety. H--
was probably killed looping a 2b, a machine
which can be looped but with a fine chance for
the pilot to kill himself. An Avro can be
looped, but it is not allowed at this School.
It is not built for that sort of thing and one
is only courting trouble if he tries it. Now
that I am past the greenhorn stage, I shall not
take any risks of getting hurt in England, any
more than I should chance getting run over by a
motor in London. Wood, who was in a bad smash,
is all right again now. His accident was due to
losing his head. I have never got excited in
the air in over 40 hours flying, and shall not
be likely to do so now.

I flew an Avro for 20 minutes the other day
with both hands in my pockets and then only took
hold of the stick because it was time to land.
Does not this speak well for the stability of
the Avro? Even if the engine stops all the
machine does is to glide slowly to earth,
keeping the correct gliding angle herself.

Central Flying School,
21st October 1917

This morning mail brought quite a Canadian
budget. I have not yet been able to follow
Babe's suggestion to photograph Brown, my
batman. When we moved out of tent, I was
unfortunate enough to lose the services of my
faithful Brown, and had to put up with the
inferior attentions of one S—— a civilian
servant. He is both lazy and incompetent and not
being a soldier, he could neither be cursed nor
threatened with incarceration in the guard room.
I stood him about, a week and then bribed the
corporal in charge of the batmen, to have old
Brown returned to me. Since then I have once
more revelled in clean boots and shiny belt and
find my belongings in their proper places and my
hot water bottle in bed on cold nights. I am no
longer allowed to oversleep in the mornings as
Brown is adamant and makes me get up in plenty
of time for my 7.30 a.m. parade.

I got a fine camels hair and wool fleece
lining for my trench coat from Burberry's,
which is a comfort, now that the weather is
getting cold. I wear it under my oilskin when
flying and in my room as a dressing gown. Worn
under my trench coat it makes a waterproof
garment chill proof as well and is fine for
motoring. We pampered people of the RFC get a
goodly amount of motoring, even with petrol at
$1.00 per gallon. Hardly a week passes but I
get two or three long rides by tender.

I seem to have finished with my beloved Avros

and am flying a Morane[15] biplane. It is not so
steady as an Avro and it will not fly alone. We
fly them to perfect ourselves in making
landings, as a Morane's probably the hardest
machine to land properly. I have been flying
them a week now and seem to have done pretty
well. I broke an axle in landing on Thursday
but that was a mere nothing. Aside from the
difficult landing, they are beautiful machines
to fly and they have a lovely engine. They are
small and in the air resemble a fish more than
a bird. Yesterday I was up in one for an hour
and 30 minutes and during my wanderings about
the country went down over Salisbury and from a
height of about a mile, viewed the old town and
its huge cathedral, set in a beautiful green
garden.

On Thursday evening, on the invitation of a
chap who went to school with me at Wellesley, I

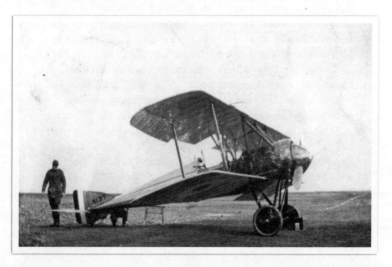

attended a small dance at a little country vicarage three miles away. Five of us went and had a pleasant evening. The following day all five of us flew over the house at various times and coming down low performed simple stunts for the amusement of the family.

Last Friday I again went by tender to Devizes to visit the dentist. I wandered about the town by myself and took one or two photographs. It is an old place and has more small inns in proportion to its population, than any other town I ever saw. I brought up at the Black Swan[16] where I had tea. We drove the twelve miles back to the school in the dark, leaving Devizes at 6.30 p.m.

Speaking of damaging my Morane the other day reminds me that Bird, Hetherington, Hemsworth and I have been responsible for probably $50,000 damage to machines since we started to fly. My contribution towards this enormous sum has been very small but does it not take your breath away? No one was hurt in any of these crashes. It does look funny to see a machine, after a bad landing, tip over and lay on her back with her wheels pointing towards the sky, or else roll over on her nose with her tail pointing straight up in the air.

Central Flying School,
28th October 1917

Last Monday my friend Bird and I heard that an
S.E. had crashed near Ludgershall. We happened
to know the girl who was to drive the tender
despatched to its assistance, and as the
weather was not good enough for flying, we went
along too. After a 10 mile ride we found the
bus on her nose in a field. The pilot was
unhurt. He had got lost and in coming down to
enquire his whereabouts, he had made a bad
landing and crashed. We left the mechanics to
load the machine on the trailer and Bird and I
and Booth the pilot adjourned to the Officer's
Mess of the 13th Battalion, Worcester Regiment
and had lunch. They treated us very well, and
we spent most of the afternoon there. We got

back to camp about 6 p.m.

I have finished with Moranes and am now
flying the wonderful S.E. 5 machine. This is
the type I am to fly in France. The first solo
was an ordeal as the tremendously powerful
Hispano-Suiza 200 h.p. motor tends all the time
to pull the machine to the right, and to
counteract this the pilot has to keep the left
rudder on all the time. I managed my first solo
without accident of any kind. These are our
fastest single seater scout machines at
present. They can fly level at 120 miles per
hour and are strong enough to be dived at 200.
The motor is heavy and consequently the machine
cannot be chucked about in the air so readily
as a Sopwith Camel. The S.E. 5 can be made to
do vertical banks, climbing turns, spins, side-
slips and loops. On account of the heavy engine
they have to fly fast through the air to keep
from dropping and consequently must be landed
at great speed, less than 70 miles an hour is
unsafe for landing. They are absolutely
inherently stable and will fly for hours with
"hands off" the controls. This was a great
comfort after a Morane, which has to be flown
by the pilot every minute. They will ramble
along at 100 miles per hour and the pilot can
warm his hands, by placing them in his pockets,
or he can open out and study a map, or make
notes, write letters or read. The cockpit is so
well enclosed and protected from the rush of
air that the pilot sits in comparative comfort
and can if necessary remove and clean his
goggles, an impossibility in a Morane.

While training in England I found that with

an S.E. 5, I could catch up to any other machine with ease and of course could run away from them too, if I so desired. No greater sport can be imagined than a practice flight with another S.E. The main object is to approach the opponent from behind. This is done either by diving from above or climbing from below so that his machine prevents him from seeing you. If one gets too close behind, the rear machine is tossed about like a cork by the wash from the other propeller. One must be careful not to get too close, as the pursuer gets out of control temporarily and the pursued is able to get away.

A record of practice flights is secured by a dummy machine gun rigidly fixed to the aeroplane. It contains in its barrel a camera and when the sights show a good position on the tail of your opponent, you press the gun trigger and if the aim is correct you have a picture of the other machine. The gun is aimed by steering your machine till your opponent's bus appears in your telescopic sight. Can you imagine anything more exciting, a cloudless day and two machines chasing each other, round and round and up and down, a mile high most of the time? I have seldom come down after a flight cold. I find the chief problem is to keep from getting too warm inside one's leather flying kit.

As we only do five hours on S.E.'s here, I shall in all probability be in France next Sunday. The Central Flying School has been a good old home to me since July and it will be quite a wrench to me to leave it.

At the Camp,
29th October 1917

On the eve of my departure for the
Expeditionary Force in France to serve in the
Royal Flying Corps, I am making a few notes
which will, I trust, be forwarded to my father
in Canada in the event of any casualty
occurring to me within the next few months.
Going as I almost certainly shall to a Scout
Squadron, I am fully aware of the hazardous
nature of the work to he done, and the almost
certainty of some mishap befalling me sooner or
later.

The present system of aerial fighting
necessitates several friendly machines always
flying in a formation or small compact group,
which reduces to a very large extent the risks
of one of their number being brought down. Even
if one should be brought down the other members
of the formation can usually see what has
happened and can give a fairly accurate report
as to whether the pilot has been killed or has
managed to land his machine fairly intact.
Consequently if I should fall during an aerial
combat, my colleagues ought to be able to
furnish a report which would relieve doubt and
possibly a long period of anxiety got those at
home.

Information concerning a casualty should be
sought from two sources:
(1) the War Office, London
(2) the Officer Commanding the Squadron,
B.E.F., France.

Risks and hazards of the RFC may be great but when one is engaged as a member of a fighting force, it is a consolation to know, that, he is one of the Senior Service of fighting armies, and a scout pilot is probably one of the highest trained and most effective units of the whole army. He sees more of what's going on than any other soldier. He is entrusted with a machine worth 3000. He does not have to put up with the heart-breaking conditions of mud and wet under which the rest of the army labour and he is extremely well paid.

In addition to this a scout pilot is, one might say, a pioneer (for the flying game is still in its infancy) in that branch of the service which will ultimately cause the final downfall of Prussian militarism with all its hateful consequences.

The machine on which I have been trained in England is the best scout machine which the British Corps at present possess.

If I am killed I should like my family to know that ever since I enlisted in 1916 my thoughts have ever been with them and while at times I have been very weary of the war, I never regretted the step I took in donning uniform.

London,
2nd November 1917

Much as I expected to be in France, the fates
took a hand in things.

After a short flight last Sunday my engine
gave a little trouble, with the result that I
made a rather bad landing, breaking the
undercarriage of my bus and bumping my head
against the back of the seat. I thought nothing
of the jolt at the time, but our doctor who
heard about it told me not to fly, for a day or
two, and about five hours later I was glad of
this, as the muscles of my neck stiffened up.
This lasted three days but has now disappeared.
The doctor is a good old sort, and hinted at
leave, which I applied for and got, so now I am
in London.

This trip to London is rather in the way of
novelty, as I am wearing my wings for the first
time, having just received my graduation
certificate from the Central Flying School. The
wings are white and are worn on the left breast
just under the pocket. They set off one's tunic
in great style.

So far I have managed to scare away the
Gothas when I come to London on leave. There
have been some pretty bad raids and one bomb
dropped recently right in Piccadilly Circus,
killed a lot of people, and made a huge hole in
the street, and smashed all the plate glass
windows in Swan & Edgars store.

*At the Camp,
10th November 1917*

Yesterday I had my first flight in 10 days and
for fear I might have forgotten how to fly or
land, I was sent up in an Avro. I got on well
enough it seems, so to-day. I was put back on
S.E.'s and had a fine hour fighting Hemsworth,
who was up in another S.E. We had a pretty good
scrap, which consisted solely of manoeuvring
for positions. I had the best buss and managed
to beat him rather badly. After we tired of
this we went and dived on trains on the Great
Western Railway. As most of them were freight
or "goods" trains, and could not do over 40
miles an hour, we found it rather slow and came
home.

Doesn't it sound thrilling to have a fast
enough mode of travel to make catching trains
dull sport?

It is now Sunday evening and I have been
resting since four o'clock. I flew all morning,
and after lunch the Canadian Officers played a
baseball game against the American Ack Emmas.
It was my first game for many months.

At the Camp,
17th November 1917

Things are rather critical and sugar and tea
are so scarce that when one is invited out for
a meal and asks for sugar for his tea, the
family produce it from some strong box and the
guest usually finds that every one else refuses
sugar, with a saint like expression on their
faces. Bacon, butter and chocolate are all dear
and hard to get at any price. Boots are a
dreadful price.

Bishop has certainly done wonders in France.
He was turned out at the Central Flying School
and is a good example of what the School can
produce. On his way back to Canada he stopped
here for a day or two and on several occasions
performed for our benefit on an S.E. 5. He did
nothing, however, that the rest of us cannot
do. He quite deserves any fuss that may be made
over him at home. He has done enough at the
front to earn a rest and I think will be given
an instructional post in England on his return.
There are so many pilots now, that after they
have done about four months in France, nearly
all are returned to England as instructors, so
I may be back here again before so very long.

These cold nights produce heavy mists in the
mornings and as a result we have no flying
before 11. Flying is not very pleasant when it
is hazy and it is hard to see objects from a
greater height than 1000 feet. Under 1000 feet
it is not safe except with careful flying and
this becomes monotonous day after day. Today I

77

went up to fly formation with my instructor. My
object was to keep as close to his machine as
possible and I managed to get pretty close. He
became disgusted with the mist and much to my
annoyance began looping the loop. Needless to
say I could hardly do this too as the machines
were too close to make it safe, so I dived and
landed. When he came down he explained that he
was looping as a signal that the weather was
too "dud' to make formation worthwhile and that
he was going back to the aerodrome.

Great interest is being taken by us in the
new Air Force Bill, which has now had its
second reading. It will create a new fighting
force separate from the Army and Navy and we
shall be neither sailors nor soldiers but
airmen, and probably will wear some new kind
of uniform.

Entry in Pilots' Flying Log Book,
17th November 1917

Grand total Solo to date, 43 hours 20 minutes.
Grand total, time in air, 63 hours minutes.

France,
24th November 1917

We left London on the "leave" train in the gray
dawn early this morning and reached the port of
embarkation (a town I well know) without event.
We had a rough crossing but as it was not
raining we remained on the top deck and managed
not to be ill, although a lot of the chaps were
pretty sick. We had a great hunt claiming our
baggage; and had quite a chance to jabber what
small amount of French we knew. Hemsworth and I
go to our Squadron tonight.

No. 60 Squadron, RFC, B.E.F.,[17]
France, 28th November 1917[18]

I have reached the Squadron which is to be my
new home for sometime to come
   I left Boulogne by train some time after
midnight and we travelled by jerks all night
long in a French railway carriage, minus
blinds, windows, doors and light. Our
destination was a small station somewhere in
Flanders and as we did not know exactly how far
away it was we had to keep a lookout after the
first four hours in case we should run past it
in the dark. I had just dozed off to sleep
again when we reached our little station. We
tumbled out and ran half a mile down the track
to the luggage van and pulled out our kit and
threw it off the train, just as it commenced to
move out again.
   The next thing was to get in touch with our
aerodrome, which we did by telephone. While
waiting for the tender we went to the village
in search of breakfast. This we found at the
Cafe France, a sort of officers' club run by a
Belgian woman. We got a fairly decent meal of
scrambled eggs, bread and coffee. The way the
French prepare coffee gives it a peculiar taste
but it is not an unpleasant one.
   When the tender came we collected our kit and
started on a long cold ride to the aerodrome,
which we reached in three quarters of an hour.
The first thing was to report to the Squadron
Commander, a Captain who last summer had been
one of my instructors. He was in temporary

command in the absence of the Major,[19] who was on leave, but has since returned. When we went to the Mess we ran into a lot more of Central Flying School boys who had been there in our time. There are about 24 officers in the Squadron and more than half of these are Canadians, so I feel quite at home. As a newcomer I shall not get much flying during the first fortnight. I shall do all I can round the aerodrome, for practice, so that when the time comes fro me to go over the line I shall know something about it.

Of all the S.E. 5 squadrons in France, we seem to have struck the best. It is one which has done exceedingly well in the past. Both the late Captain Ball[20] and Major Bishop belonged to it and there have been fewer casualties than in any other similar squadron. Having had so few, the chaps have been in the game a long time and so have had wide experience and this is bound to be of inestimable benefit to new people. The aerodrome is a good 20 miles behind the line, and is practically immune from shell fire. None have landed anywhere near for months.

I share a hut with three others and we have lots of room. The huts are like half a barrel laid on the ground; the curved roof is corrugated iron and the ends are wood. We have several tables, comfortable chairs, our camp beds and innumerable rugs on the floor. A coal stove and an oil stove give plenty of heat, and petrol lamps give excellent light. I have not had such comfortable permanent quarters since leaving Canada and yet we are within sound range of the guns which never cease. I was able to bring over practically every article of kit I possessed. An infantry officer would have had to leave nine-tenths of it behind.

One great comfort is that here we can wear just exactly what we like. We can come to breakfast in pyjamas and wear comfortable old clothes all day long. Puttees I am discarding for good and in their place will wear long stockings. They have always been an abomination, as their tightness stops circulation and induces cold. We do not wear belts and can fly in sweaters. In fact it will be a long summer holiday with lots of excitement thrown in. Leave comes round every three months, and lasts for fourteen days.

*No. 60 Squadron, RFC, B.E.F.,
France, 29th November 1917.*

Owing to bad weather there has been practically
no work to do and while I have been at my new
home nearly a week I have not been over the
lines yet.

My first struggle with the French language
was mainly concerned with ordering meals and
feeble requests for note paper and enquiries
for trains and the location of towns. My
companion knew absolutely no French so I had to
do all the talking: I can hardly realize that
at last I am actually in the war zone, so
comfortable are we here and so happy. The
others in the Mess are all congenial, more than
half are Canadians and many of them I knew
previously.

I have not been assigned to any particular
machine since crossing, and have not even had a
flight, but it will be a single seater scout
machine with a 200 h.p. motor which will drive
it 120 miles an hour. It sounds pretty fast,
but that speed is slow compared with the rate
which it can be dived, 230 miles an hour can be
done with safety. My Squadron is one of the
best of its kind and I am glad to say has been
remarkably free from casualties. It has
countless Huns to its credit.

*No 60 Squadron, RFC B.E.F.,
France, 2nd December 1917*

Sunday morning again and it is a week since
Hemsworth[21] and I arrived at No. 60 Squadron.
The time has passed quickly, and neither of us
has been in the air since we left the good old
Central Flying School.

I am sitting alone in the Mess as I write,
bathed in a strong odour of banana oil. The men
are "doping" our white muslin windows with a
solution used for making a wind and waterproof
surface on aeroplane wings and we thought it
would be a good scheme to put this stuff over
our windows to keep out the wind. It contains a
large percentage of banana oil, hence the
smell. My own hut is a sporty place, and
instead of white cloth for windows we have
substituted real glass which Crompton,[22] one of
the inmates procured in a stealthy manner from
some unknown source.

Our hut is very comfortable. You never saw
such a fine collection of rugs. For the first
time since leaving home (barring hotels) I have
been able to walk the floor comfortably in bare
feet. At night, when our stove is roaring we
are fine and warm but towards morning when
getting up time comes it is pretty cold. Before
leaving England I got a fleece sleeping bag
from my tailor, and I find it useful already.

Our aerodrome (between Cassel and Hazebrouck)
is a large one, and this is a good thing, as
landing an S.E. in a small aerodrome is quite a
problem. We share it with two other squadrons,

and another is expected shortly. Each squadron
has its own Mess, so we do not see much of the
others, but they all seem friendly and a nice
lot of fellows. Since I came, one of our oldest
pilots has gone back to England and a new one
has arrived, so I am no longer the junior
member of the Mess.

There are no end of dogs about the aerodrome.
Our Mess has a few special ones of different
breeds, and with such names as Lobo, Nigger,
Rastus, Bride and one "HispanoSuiza" so-called
because our engines bear the same name. His
chief accomplishment is yelping in order to get
into our hut on cold nights. In reading the
Squadron Orders yesterday I came across a
paragraph forbidding pilots from conveying dogs
to England in aeroplanes. There is a law
prohibiting the bringing of dogs into the
United Kingdom.

To add to the comfort of the Mess, besides
dogs, we have a fairly good piano and a
gramophone. Every time any one goes on leave he
brings back a few records, and the collection
is now quite large.

The change from the school to here has been
for the worse, as far as batmen go. I shall
never be able to get another like old Brown. My
present man is named Hazeldene, and just now he
is languishing in the guard room as a result of
having been found drunk yesterday.

The hours for actual flying are of necessity
short on account of the shortness of daylight.
Consequently we get lots time for exercise,
most of which consists of kicking a rugby ball
around the aerodrome. It is about the best way

of keeping warm these cold days.

Our tenders frequently run to St. Omer and even as far as Boulogne, so when not flying there are chances of seeing these places. It does seem funny to be able to go from practically the trenches to Boulogne (within sight of England) almost any time we want to. We in the RFC are about the only people who can do this.

When artillery horses are in need of a rest they are sent back from the front line. We have two or three at the Squadron and I shall probably get some riding if I can pluck up courage enough to try.

It is bound to be muddy here before the winter is over, at present everything is dry. In preparation for later we have "duck-boards" or wooden slat walks laid down between all the huts, the Mess, the hangars, etc. On a dark night is rather a problem to keep on these boards.

All the heavy labour in this part of France is now being done by Chinese coolies brought specially from China for this purpose. They are enlisted as soldiers and wear a peculiar blue padded uniform. They are employed around the aerodrome levelling ground, putting sand bags about the huts as a protection against bombs, making roads and paths, etc. They are terribly interested in our phonograph and if we leave the door open they almost come in. To keep them out, the interpreter has painted a large sign in Chinese characters, and it sticks up in front of the Mess and gives it quite an oriental appearance.

Moving picture shows are given every night or
so in a Church Army Hut in the Camp. We had
several good films last night. It hardly seems
at all like war yet.

France,
3rd December 1917

I am still merely watching operations from the
ground. Two fresh pilots have been posted to
the Squadron since Hemsworth and I arrived and
we shall probably commence flying tomorrow, if
the weather is suitable.

Great interest is being shown out here at the
coming General Election in Canada and the
authorities are endeavouring to have every
Canadian register his vote. Quite contrary to
Army precedent and regulations, the authorities
are openly urging every one to vote against
Laurier. Most of us share this view, but it is
interesting to see the officials of an Army in
the field canvassing votes for one party.

The Canadians are no longer near us. I
imagine they needed a rest badly after their
recent push.

The Squadron boasts 16 canines at present.
The Officers' Mess possesses five. We are very
proud of them. Besides these we have six pigs,
and 25 hens. There is no shortage of eggs about
the Mess.

France,
9th December 1917

Since last Sunday I have been waiting, waiting, waiting for a flight and not till last Thursday did I get it. The day was cloudy and the visibility poor. Hemsworth and I were to have a practice flight and we spent about 20 minutes at it. When we finished I had lost sight of the aerodrome and so had he, for I could see him flying aimlessly one way and then another, diving on one hill and then on several more. As our aerodrome is near to a town perched on a high hill,[23] I knew what he was looking for but none of the hills seemed to be the right one. After that he turned and flew east for a time and although I knew such a course would taking us into Hunland, I followed, deciding to go with him as far as the trenches and then turn west again; just our side of the line I spotted a town which I recognised from the great relief map we had at Oxford. It is a town which has undergone more shelling than any other during the whole war.[24] I never saw such a sight of desolation. Nothing but shell holes in all directions. Practically all the buildings in ruins, and every now and then a shell would burst in the desolate City with a blinding flash. Of course I could hear nothing of the explosion. I know my way back to the aerodrome and felt much relieved, as it is most undignified to get lost on one's first flip. I opened my engine and soon caught up to the other machine, and signalled Hemsworth to turn

around and follow me. We were at the aerodrome
25 minutes later. The flight took place last
Thursday. I have not been in the air since
owing to a temporary shortage of machines.

The Times of yesterday mentioned a terrible
explosion in Halifax which seems to have done
enormous damage.

The little town, near our aerodrome, perched
on a high hill, has a fine square, from which a
beautiful church can be seen, and the square and
streets are cobbled. The road which leads into
the town from the east enters through a short
tunnel which emerges right into the square
itself. When I was last there several howitzer
batteries were coming from the line for a rest
and the caterpillar tractors, which haul these
huge guns, were grunting and chugging from the
tunnel into the town and through it, making for
some spot further to the rear. All units which
come out of the trenches for a rest are sent far
enough back to be out of earshot of the guns.
The Casino at the highest part of the town is
devoted to military purposes. From it a
wonderful view of the western front may be had,
puffs of smoke in the distance captive sausage
observation balloons aeroplanes and roads
teeming with hundreds and hundreds of motor
lorries slowly crawling along. A batch of
miserable looking German prisoners were engaged
in cleaning the streets. Their appearance gave
the impression that they must have been reduced
to sorry straits before capture, as they all
looked white, pinched and sickly. I think they
are pretty fairly treated by our people and
certainly given enough to eat.

Speaking of food reminds me that we do pretty
well in our Mess. I quote from our ordinary
dinner menu: Soup, mock turtle, toast; Fish,
grilled sole, mustard sauce; Entree, beefsteak,
pastry, boiled potatoes, green peas; Sweets,
stewed prunes, cornstarch pudding, biscuits,
cheese, coffee.

We have the correct number of machines, six
in each flight and there are three flights, A.
B. and C. I am in B. flight. There are 18
pilots, an equipment officer who is also
Quartermaster, a Recording Officer (adjutant)
and the Commanding Officer. So we have 22 in
our Mess.

Lunch is served at one o'clock. Sometimes I
have spent the afternoons walking into the
nearby town. Tea is at four p.m. and now it is
dark at that time. After tea we read or play
cards till dinner at 7.30. After dinner some
music. By the way, we have a rag time band,
composed of a piano, a snare drum, two sets of
bones, a triangle and brass cymbals and an auto
horn. It is "some" band. We all go to bed
fairly early.

France,
15th December 1917

I can hardly express what a wonderful thing
flying is, and what a hold it gets on one. I am
having the time of my life. I trained for
nearly seven months in England and spent two of
them studying aeronautics in Oxford University.
My actual practical instruction in flying took
place in Upavon, and there spent five of the
happiest months of my life.

Over here things are fine too. Aside from
flying we get lots of motoring, football and
even riding. Certainly it pays to go to the war
on wings.

France,
16th December 1917

The past week has been an easy one for the
Squadron. I have only been in the air a few
times. Quite recently a certain town not far
off was under shell fire for two days. On the
first fine day after this we sent up machines
to a great height above the town, in order to
catch the Hun airmen, who we felt certain would
come over to take photographs of the damage
done. Sure enough one solitary Hun came over
but I think he got the fright of his life for
three of our machines chased him all the way
back to Hunland, but were unable to bring him
down. He did not get his photographs though.

I came in a few minutes ago from a game of
football which our Squadron played against No
57 Squadron. We were pretty badly beaten but
had a lot of good exercise out of it.

When cavalry horses up in front need a rest
they are sent back for a few months to units
well back from the trenches. We have three at
the aerodrome and the day yesterday I plucked
up courage and went for my first ride. I
expected to be chucked off, but by hanging on
with one hand to the saddle, I got an idea of
how to trot, and before the afternoon was out I
had done twelve miles, had several canters and
a good gallop and managed to stay on all the
time. During our ride we passed through the
heavy traffic of a large town, where snorting
lorries and puffing caterpillar tractors made
the horses nervous and unpleasantly lively.

When I got back I learned that I had been riding the liveliest of the three beasts, which has given me confidence for my next attempt.

As I write it is 6 p.m. on Sunday, There is a roaring fire in the stove. Five chaps are playing cards and one other is reading on his bed. Every two weeks or so when I am an orderly officer, I censor the mail for the NCOs and men. We of course censor our own letters.

France,
17th December 1917

I had a chance to go to St. Omer and one of the
things I wanted to buy was a coal shovel for
the stove in our hut. After poking through the
darkened streets I found what seemed to be an
iron monger's shop but could not remember the
French for "shovel" although I knew what coal
was "charbon". Hoping that Madame might
understand some English I repeated the English
word "shovel" several times coupling it with
"charbon" and waited developments. She
triumphantly appeared in a minute or two with a
toy horse and coal cart and seemed quite
surprised when I assured her that I was not in
need of a "cheval".

Have not been doing much work lately, chiefly
because of bad weather. This morning I did start
off on an offensive patrol, but came limping
back twenty minutes later with engine trouble,
and barely managed to get into the aerodrome.

Entry in Pilot's Flying Log Book, 18th December 1917

First patrol over lines, nine enemy aeroplanes seen, four engaged, time 7.25 a.m., absent one hour and 20 minutes on an S.E. 5.

Christmas Day 1917

Deeply regret to inform you
2/Lt. R. W. Maclennan, RFC,
60 Squadron, died of wounds
December twenty-third.
The Army Council express
their sympathy.

aL

CASUALTY CARD.

Tests completed _____
Went overseas _____

Rank, Name and Unit _McLennan. Lieut. R.V._

_____ _Cenral Test ana R.A.C.Co. Service_ _____ At Time of Accident) _Pilot._
Employed as ...)

Graduated as ___ _9-n-_ ___ on (date) _____

Date Report Received and Official Reference.	Date of Casualty.	Where occurred.	Type of Machine.	Nature and Cause of Accident.	Result of Accident.	Name of other Occupant of Machine.	Remarks.
R.S.Dn. 21.0419/2. 29.12. 7							

Next of Kin
R.J. McLennan (Father)
Kent Buildings

Army Form B.103c.

H 43; W3165—R1811 10,009 -5/17 HWV(B:10)
192—M3009 15,000 10/17

CASUALTY FORM—OFFICERS.

DATE OF PROMOTION (London Gazette)		Christian Names		Surname
		R	W	MACLENNAN

	Temporary	Permanent	Regiment	Branch of Service	Agent or Banker
Lieut	✓			General List	Date of joining R.F.C.
			Married or Single	Date of Birth	Next-of-Kin and Address	Date of leaving R.F.C.

DATE OF REPORT	PARTICULARS	DATE OF CASUALTY	AUTHORITY AND FROM WHOM RECEIVED
	Embarked_____	24³/₇	W.O. List W.E 24⁴/₇
	Disembarked_____		
25⁴/₇	Posted to Nº. 60 Squadron	25⁴/₇	B.213. 60 Sqdr.
16⁹/₇	To be Flying Officer + confirmed in rank	18⁸/₇	L.G.
24⁷/₇	Killed in action	23²⁴/₇	Summ 1208. G.O.C. R.F.C.
4/8	Buried at Hazebrouck M. Cem.		D.A.A.G.2.
	(Rev. G.R. Trussell, att 15 bS (undated) C/7978)		Loc. List 18975
29⁷/₇	Admitted (Burns. Effect of Heat)	23⁷/₇	E.D.5712. 15 bbS.
---	Died	23¹²/₇	—— ——

[P.T.O.

Name in full _Maclennan, Roderick Ward_   University year and degree (if any) _B.A. 1914._

Home address (Rod. J. Maclennan) _30 Murray St. Toronto, Ont. Pres._

Date and Place of enlistment _Jan 1916 Kingston_

Rank on enlistment _Private (Reinforcements)_   _Died of wounds_

Promotions (if any) _Sergt.(Prov.)_
Staff Sergt   Flight Lieut. R.F.C.
_& C.A.M.C_

Company and Battalion _No. 5 Can. Stat. Hospital (Queen's)_

or other unit _Cairo, Egypt_   Official Number _535.405_

Remarks: _Military Hospital. Shorncliffe (since June 1916)._
Died of Wounds Dec. 1917. See "Canada" Feb. 2/1918. p.35.
Journal * * 20. Jan 8/18.

101

London, From a home where Maclennan
had called shortly before he left
for France.

Oh you know how truly grieved and shocked we feel at
the terrible news just come today. It is almost
impossible to believe that that strong looking,
bright young creature has left this world when so
lately, so lately it seems, he was so happy and full
of life and energy. He told me to tell you how he
had grown, so tall and broad shouldered, that he
hardly thought you would know him again. We spoke of
all the wonders of the Universe that have been
discovered since I was born, of the number even
since he was born and I said I thought it was proof
of how our Heavenly Father was educating us for a
Higher life than this when we shall learn even more
of science and beauty and love and truth; and how
God might have told man all at once but he gave him
the joy of using his God-like powers to discover
electricity, wireless telegraphy, everything we know
and your dear son looked so reverend and thoughtful
and said:

"Oh yes, it is true, how we have
progressed, how we have learned but how much
we have still to learn even here. You can't
think what it is to be high up in the sky,
what thoughts one has".

Notes

1. Netheravon in Wiltshire.
2. Maurice Farman Shorthorn.
3. Upavon in Wiltshire.
4. Believed to be Major Joseph D Atkinson who had previously flown with 29 Squadron; he would later be awarded the Air Force Cross in 1919.
5. Maurice Farman Shorthorn.
6. AVRO 504.
7. Reference to two of Sopwith's fighter aircraft.
8. Presumably at Milk Hill north of Alton Barnes.
9. America entered the First World War in April 1917.
10. Reference to the Gotha and Zeppelin attacks on London.
11. Village immediately north of Upavon.
12. Lieutenant G W Hemsworth would survive the war.
13. Village due south of Upavon.
14. Louis Strange DSO MC DFC (1891-1966) was one of the pioneers of military aviation in Great Britain. He obtained his flying licence in August 1913 and quickly joined the RFC where, following the outbreak of war, he was credited with developing 'air fighting'. He served with 5, 23 and 45 Squadrons and survived the war. He was active as a pilot in the Second World War.
15. Morane-Saulnier BB.
16. The Black Swan still exists and can be found in Market Street.
17. British Expeditionary Force.
18. 60 Squadron was based at that time at Ste Marie Capelle near Hazebrouck in northern France.
19. Major C K C Patrick DSO DFC MC and Bar.
20. Captain Albert Ball had been killed in action 7 May 1917 with 56 Squadron. He had amassed 44 aerial kills and had been highly decorated, including the Victoria Cross.
21. The same Hemsworth who trained with him at CFS.
22. Lieutenant H D Crompton would survive the War.
23. Cassel.
24. Ypres in Belgium.

Photograph Credits

Page 5   Roderick Ward Maclennan. www.queensu.ca
Page 9   Maclennan's medical record. www.queensu.ca
Page 16   A Maurice Farman Shorthorn. Via Andy Thomas
Page 27   Upavon Officers Mess. Aldon Ferguson
Page 27   The entrance hall at Upavon Officers Mess. Aldon Ferguson
Page 33   An Avro 504K. Via Andy Thomas
Page 35   A Royal Aircraft Factory B.E.2. This is a 2C example. Chris Goss
Page 69   A Morane-Saulnier BB. Via Andy Thomas
Page 72   A Royal Aircraft Factory S.E.5. Chris Goss
Page 99   Second Lieutenant Roderick Ward Maclennan's grave. The War Graves Photographic Project
Page 100   Casualty card. www.queensu.ca
Page 101   Maclennan's Officer Casualty Form. www.queensu.ca
Page 101   The service record of Roderick Ward Maclennan. www.queensu.ca

Please return this book on or before the date marked above. If over-
due a charge will be made in accordance with library regulations.

The period of loan may be extended (once only by post or telephone) if the book is not required by another reader. To renew,
please quote either YOUR TICKET NUMBER (at computerised
libraries), or AUTHOR, TITLE, DATE DUE and

▼———— THIS NUMBER ————▼

11012813   3

North Yorkshire County Library

NORTH YORKSHIRE COUNTY LIBRARY

Stockton's Quest

Dan Stockton, a train conductor, has the misfortune to be mistaken for Cy Monk – the notorious outlaw and most reviled man in the West. Uncannily similar in appearance, Stockton is even identified by the sheriff as the man who once abandoned a wagon train he was escorting through Indian country, resulting in the bloody slaughter of its settlers. Wanted and on the run, Stockton's troubles mount as he is forced to become a jail-breaker and a bank-robber.

When it doesn't look as if things will ever get any better he finally convinces an army colonel of his true identity.

Even then, he must face the real criminals – gun-runners who won't hesitate to shoot him down. Can Stockton win through?

Stockton's Quest

SKEETER DODDS

A Black Horse Western

ROBERT HALE · LONDON

ISBN 0 7090 7486 7

Robert Hale Limited
Clerkenwell House
Clerkenwell Green
London EC1R 0HT

Typeset by
Derek Doyle & Associates, Liverpool.
Printed and bound in Great Britain by
Antony Rowe Limited, Wiltshire

PROLOGUE

The angry man growled, 'Ya've got more yella in ya than a damn daffodil, mister!' Dan Stockton sipped his drink and did his best to ignore the belligerent man. 'Ya deaf?' the man wearing a faded Union tunic bellowed, crowding Stockton.

'Leave it, Ned,' the man's partner counselled. 'He ain't worth wastin' a bullet on, I say.'

The incensed man shrugged off his partner's hand on his shoulder. 'This whore's spit ran out on that wagon train that got massacred at Begley Creek. And I aim to square the account for them folk, Andy.'

'You've got a whiskey-softened brain, Ned,' Andy cautioned. 'That hands Monk the advantage.'

Dan Stockton hated folk to think of him as Cy Monk, a mangy cur who deserved skinning alive. But he had been born with a dial uncannily like Monk's, and it was that unfortunate stroke of misfortune which had brought him to the no-consequence town of Thunder Ridge.

'I could outdraw him ten times as drunk,' Ned boasted.

'No you couldn't, mister,' Stockton said quietly, his grey eyes as hard as flint, his tone pitched to reach only Ned. 'Take your friend's advice. Leave me be. I'm not looking for trouble.'

His challenger sneered. 'Wan' me to turn my back for ya, yella?'

Stockton addressed the man called Andy: 'Haul your firebrand friend out of here while he's still sucking air.'

Andy shuffled nervously. 'C'mon, Ned. Let's vamoose.'

Ned spun round on his partner. 'Leave me be I tell ya!' He stepped back from the bar, settling the poorly-cared-for six gun on his right hip. 'Scum like you, Monk, should be cut down without a chance like the rabid mongrel you are. But I'm goin' to give you a chance to draw.'

Andrew Collins, the owner of the Silver Arrow saloon withdrew from the poker game he was engaged in. 'You're all liquored, Ned. Go on home to Sarah. She'll be fretting for you.'

Ned said bitterly, 'Yella, too! I wouldn't 'spect nothin' else from you, Collins. You bein' a Reb, an' all.'

'The war is over and done with, Ned,' Collins said calmly, though the red spots on his cheeks showed the anger inside him. 'Time to put it to rest.'

'I'm goin' to kill this bastard, Collins,' Ned snarled. He shoved his whiskey-flushed face in the saloon owner's. 'You think I can't take this yella-belly?'

'Ned,' Andy pleaded.

The angry man's shove sent his partner flying across the poker table which Collins had vacated. Those holding losing cards took the opportunity to grab their share of the pot scattering across the saloon floor. As a result, an angry skirmish broke out, momentarily diverting attention away from the stand-off at the bar.

'Ya're a yella coyote, Monk!' Ned screamed. 'Draw that damn gun! Or beg me to let you live.'

Stockton put his glass down on the bar and stepped back. 'You must be really anxious to become a harp player, mister. Push again, and I'll kill you for sure.'

Dan was relieved to see a paleness wash through the redness of the man's face. It meant that he was having second thoughts. Stockton wished that he could explain his reason for masquerading as Cy Monk, the notorious outlaw. But if he did that, the hell's trail he had ridden to Thunder Ridge would all be for nothing, and the many lives that depended on the success of his mission would be lost.

Though he'd regret having to draw iron, he had to maintain his role as Cy Monk until the varmints he had come to Thunder Ridge to nail showed

7

their hand. He had only been in town for an hour, but he supposed that that was long enough to invite trouble. Begley Creek, the scene of the Indian massacre which had got Ned so riled up, was one of the most odious treacheries in the West's long litany of infamy. Cy Monk had taken settlers' dollars to see their wagon train through Indian territory and had deserted them, leaving them roll smack into an Apache ambush.

'Walk away, mister,' Dan told his challenger.

Stockton hoped that the man called Ned would. Because there was no guarantee that he could outdraw him. Cy Monk would. But he was not Cy Monk. And he was no gunslick either.

'Are ya goin' for that iron or not, Monk?' Ned barked.

Andrew Collins stepped in again with a welcome compromise. 'Why don't you go home and sober up, Ned,' he said in the svelte tone of the professional negotiator, which every Western saloon owner had to be. 'Come back tomorrow. Finish Monk then, if he's still around.'

Andy jumped at the chance to extricate himself and his partner from danger. 'Mr Collins is makin' real good sense, Ned. Tomorrow you'll easily kill this toerag.'

Ned made a garrulous show of backing down, but there was no mistaking the relief in his eyes. He had pushed too far, and was grateful to get the chance to back out.

'Tomorrow, Monk. Be on the street at high noon.'

'I'll be there,' Dan barked, keeping up the pretence, wisely allowing Ned to save face.

The batwings crashed open. Marshal Sam Cade stepped through the shuddering doors toting a Greener, his eyes flashing to Dan Stockton.

'The trouble is done and dusted, Marshal,' Collins said.

'Until tomorrow, Collins,' Ned reminded the saloon owner.

Although he had only been in town for an hour, it was, Dan reckoned, a long time before the marshal had put in an appearance. He had counted on being ordered out of town as soon as he hitched his horse to the rail outside the Silver Arrow, and had been thinking up ways of hanging on until the purpose of his visit to Thunder Ridge was completed. However, Cade had not put in an appearance, though he had watched his arrival through the law office window with a keen interest. Strange behaviour for a lawman.

'Sure, Ned,' the saloon owner said, snake-oil slick. 'You see Ned home safely, Andy.'

'Sure will, Mr Collins.'

Andy pulled Ned along with him.

Now, Dan figured, Cade would order him out of town, and the confrontation with Ned would override any reason he could come up with for staying. He cursed silently that all the trouble he had been through to reach Thunder Ridge was going to be wasted.

Collins said, 'Drop by for a drink later, Sam. Maybe a little poker, too.'

Cade nodded and left.

Dan Stockton could not believe his good fortune.

'Pour this gentleman another beer on the house,' the saloon owner ordered the barkeep.

'Mighty generous,' Dan said.

Dan pondered on Collins' exchange with the marshal, and there was no doubting who the boss-man was. The saloon owner returned to the poker table. Stockton finished his drink, and drifted out of the Silver Arrow. Outside, he looked along the dusty street and wondered how long he'd have to wait for the men he had come to find to reveal themselves.

Then the nagging worry that had bothered him returned to haunt him. What if Thunder Ridge was not the right town? What if the conversation he had belatedly eavesdropped on, where he had heard mention of Thunder Ridge, was to do with something entirely different to the purpose of his mission?

'Well,' Dan Stockton murmured, 'only time will tell.'

The trail to Thunder Ridge begins. . . .

CHAPTER ONE

'All 'board!'

Dan Stockton's voice carried bell-clear along the platform over the hissing steam coming from the locomotive. The train rolling, he nimbly hopped on board, the evidence of long familiarity with the procedure evident in his gait. Stockton slammed the door of the conductor's caboose shut before he let dissatisfaction show on his face; a face that was a strange and unique mixture of cowboy and slicker. His dissatisfaction stemmed from the drudgery of his job. Ending up as a train conductor was not something he had planned on; his plans had been much bigger than that. He had seen himself raising fine horses that would make the man who bred them proud. Instead he had found himself drifting; a drifter among drifters. One of the many men who had, once the fighting had stopped, found themselves at a loose end, skilled only in killing.

'There's enough land out West for a man to take the rest of his days to reach its end,' a crusty old sergeant who had roamed the West before the war, had told him. 'And all the wild horses a man could break and breed.

'Tell ya, son. If I had the spit in me, that's where I'd be headed once all this nonsense is over and done with.'

It was on that balmy night, lit by the light of a full Georgian moon a couple of weeks before the end of the war, listening to the sergeant tell his tales about what he'd seen out West, that Dan Stockton had made his decision. When he told the grizzled sergeant of that decision, he had smiled and said:

'It's right what you're doin', young fella. Wish I was doin' it with ya.'

'You can,' Dan had said, bursting at the seams with enthusiasm. 'We'll have pay coming when the book on this shindig is finally closed. If we pool our resources we'd have ourselves a good start, wouldn't we?'

'I guess,' the sergeant said, his tired eyes lighting with a fire as glowing as a convert's. But after a moment's dreaming he had doubted, 'D'ya think we could, son?'

'Don't see why not,' was Dan's encouraging reply. 'You know horses, and I've got a strong enough back to do most of the work. What's to stop us?'

14

'Nothin', I reckon,' the old sergeant had said. Nothin' at all, son.'

'That'll be Dan from now on, Sergeant.'

'Dan it is.' He vigourously shook Dan's hand. 'Jackdaw, they call me,' he said. 'And you can too, if you want.'

'Jackdaw?'

'Ain't a proper name,' the sergeant said. 'But it's sure better than Yeoville, the name my folk gave me at baptism.'

'Yeoville?' Dan tried, but failed to hold back his laughter.

'Don't you go tellin' no one now, ya hear?' the sergeant pleaded, regretting his confidence. 'How would I keep muster over this ragbag outfit if they knew my name was Yeoville.'

Dan tested the sound of the name again. 'Yeoville. . . .' He was even more amused. 'Yeoville what?'

'None of your damn business!'

'If we're to be partners there can be no secrets between us, Yeo . . . I mean, Jackdaw,' Dan corrected, withering under the sergeant's glacial gaze.

'Well . . .' the old-timer looked round him.

'There's not a soul awake but us,' Dan encouraged him.

'Fancy,' he murmured.

Dan grinned. 'Yeoville Fancy.'

'Shush!'

15

The sergeant's eyes flashed around the sleeping camp.

Dan said with blunt honesty, 'No wonder you want to be called Jackdaw.'

'Yeoville, dammit. Never could figger out how my folk come up with such a Fancy Dan handle,' the sergeant groused. 'Been a millstone round my darn neck all my life, when legal things like joinin' this man's army needed my proper mark on paper.'

As the raw country beyond the conductor's window passed by, Dan Stockton fondly recalled that night on the edge of a Georgia swamp. Then, sadly, his mind turned to a rain-soaked night not far from where Jackdaw and he had planned their future, their dreams getting bigger as the sleepless night wore on towards dawn.

The makeshift watering hole was a tent sagging under the weight of the rain, but it was the only place where the exhausted Union soldiers could go to celebrate the fall of the Confederacy.

'Ya comin' 'long, Dan?' Jackdaw had asked. 'The whiskey will rot your guts, but they've got real pretty doves,' he tempted.

Dan lay back on his cot and sighed. 'Another three days and we'll be on our way, Jackdaw. To breed them high-stepping critters you've been filling my head with. Liquor and women aren't any match for dreaming about that.'

For a moment Jackdaw was caught up in Dan

Stockton's mooning, but his thirst and the gnawing in his groin soon took precedence over his dreaming.

'Don't you be late home,' Dan scolded him as he left.

Laughing, Jackdaw flung back, 'Sure won't, Mama. But don't you lose any sleep worryin' your pretty head now, ya hear.'

The night had not counted off many of its hours, when word came that Jackdaw had fallen foul of a gambler and had caught lead. He was not dead. But when Dan saw him in the hospital tent, he wished that he was. Backshot, Jackdaw's spine had been shattered, leaving him with useless sticks of legs.

'The doc says that I'm goin' to be a cripple for the rest of m' life, Dan. Don't reckon I'd want that. Bein' dependent, an' all.'

Understanding the drift of Jackdaw's thoughts, Dan had done his best to change his mind. But eventually, he left his pistol nearby.

'You're still goin' after that dream we've been dreamin', ain't ya?' Jackdaw wanted to know.

'Doesn't seem as much fun any more, Jackdaw,' Dan had replied, his spirits low.

Jackdaw had grabbed him by the hand and dragged him towards him, his eyes fiery with determination. 'Now you listen and listen good, Dan Stockton. Even if I made the trip with ya, in a coupla years I'd be wormbait. But you're a young

17

one, with lotsa years 'head o' ya. You go and breed them hosses for old Yeoville Fancy, ya hear me now?'

To calm him, Dan had promised that he would.

Jackdaw grinned. 'You keep that promise, or so help me I'll haunt ya.'

'Sure I will. And I'll call the place Jackdaw Ranch, too.'

Exhausted, the old sergeant fell back on his pillow. He took a wad of dollar bills from under his mattress and pressed them into Dan's hand, overriding his objections. 'I ain't got no use for them,' he told Dan. He smiled, the light in his eyes dimming. 'Jackdaw Ranch, huh.'

Dan hurried from the hospital tent, obeying Jackdaw's order not to look back.

'Because the future's 'head o' ya, son. Waitin' for you to take it by the scruff of the neck.'

He had not gone far in the downpour, when his steps faltered on hearing the boom of a gun from the hospital tent. He showed his face to the rain to hide his tears.

Weary of spirit, Dan decided to stroll through the train. 'Ugly critter aren't you,' he commented on the Wanted poster of a train robber by the name of Spike Ross, pinned on the wall of the conductor's caboose. He was walking through the third coach when out of the blue, a woman who had been sizing him up from the second he had entered the coach, sprang out of her seat and

18

slapped him hard across the face.

'Coward!' she screamed, and announced to the surprised passengers, 'This man is Cy Monk.'

There was a stunned silence, before a man leapt from his seat full of righteous indignation. 'The Cy Monk of Begley Creek notoriety, ma'am?'

'The same sidewinder,' the woman confirmed.

The passengers turned cold, unfriendly eyes on Dan.

'My name's not Monk,' Dan protested. 'My name's Dan Stockton, ma'am.'

'Hah!' the woman snorted. 'Change your name if you will, Monk. But you can't change your damn spots!' Dan felt her hot spittle on his face as she came toe-to-toe with him. 'You deserted more than fifty souls and let them face the Apache all on their own at Begley Creek. May you rot in hell for that!'

'My name is Dan Stockton,' Dan repeated, seeking believers among the passengers, but finding only accusing and hostile faces staring back at him.

'We should just stop the train and hang him right now,' a galoot of a man said.

'Good idea,' another man agreed.

Dan felt hands grabbing him. He struggled, but the sheer force of numbers pinned him down. A voice filled with authority intervened:

'Leave him be.' The men, their blood up, were about to argue with the man, when a six gun flashed in his hand. 'I said leave him be.'

'You heard that he's Cy Monk, didn't you?' the

leader of the pack asked the quietly spoken interventionist.

'I heard. And I'll admit that this feller has Monk's dial and thatch all right. But as a lawman, I've got to be certain,' he touched his hat to the woman, 'that he is who you say he is, ma'am.'

'How're you going to do that?' the galoot enquired of the lawman.

'Tonto Crossing is the next stop. Right?'

Dan nodded.

'The sheriff there is a fella called Tom Healy. Used to wear a badge in Twin Pines, the town nearest to Begley Creek. Hunted Monk for over two years after the Apache massacre. He'll know for sure if this fella is Cy Monk.'

The galoot said, 'We hang him in Tonto Crossing if Healy says that he's Monk. Agreed?'

The marshal stood firm. 'Due process of law will apply, mister.'

Grumbling, the men handed Dan over to the lawman. His relief was palpable. Safe, in as much as he could be in the lawman's protection if mob law broke out, Dan once more contradicted the common belief that he was the notorious outlaw Cy Monk.

'Save your breath, Monk,' a fleshy-nosed man with mottled cheeks growled, swinging a fist that narrowly missed Dan.

'How those poor creatures must have suffered,' a diminutive woman wailed.

'How many times do I have to tell you . . .' Dan sighed. 'Oh, what's the point. Your ears are closed.'

'You're Monk all right,' his female accuser spat.

The men who had wanted to haul him off to the nearest tree again surged forward.

'Marshal Saul Gordon,' the lawman introduced himself, thumbing the hammer of his .45. 'Now you folk let this affair to the law for fixing.' He said to Dan, 'If you're not Monk, then that dial of yours was a real stroke of bad luck, mister.'

Dan Stockton shrugged. 'I can't do anything about that, Marshal. It's the one I was born with.'

'And maybe the one that will get you hanged,' the lawman intoned.

The time it took for the train to reach Tonto Crossing was not long, but for Dan Stockton it was a lifetime. The second the train stopped, the galoot led the party from the station to the sheriff's office, informing everyone as they went, despite Gordon's warnings, that Dan was the infamous Cy Monk. By the time they reached the law office a sizeable crowd had gathered, which was getting bigger by the second.

'What're we waitin' for?' one incensed woman screamed. 'We've got a hangin' tree right at the end of Main.'

'You're right, Mamie,' a man called out above the baying of the crowd, rapidly turning to a lynch mob. 'He's Monk all right. Came face-to-face with him when I was nursing cows for an outfit in Colorado. Monk was working at the ranch as a *persuader*, as the boss would put it. Meaning he forced people out who stood in the way of Ned Cole's ambition to own the entire darn county.' Then he added, damningly: 'Saw him shoot a widder woman, while her ten-year-old boy looked on.'

The man spat contemptuously at Dan.

Dan Stockton knew that a lynching was imminent.

The crowd closed around Dan. Saul Gordon's exhortations to stay back made no dent on the howling mob's determination to drag Dan to the hanging tree. A man wearing a sheriff's badge put in an appearance. The shotgun he toted was a real comfort to Dan, but his relief was short-lived. The Tonto Crossing sheriff fixed unfriendly eyes on him.

'By all that's holy,' he grated. 'If it ain't Cy Monk!'

CHAPTER TWO

'No use huffing and puffing,' the Tonto Crossing sheriff told Dan, when he again protested that he was not Cy Monk. 'I'd know you anywhere, Monk.'

Stockton switched his plea to Gordon, whose response was a resigned shrug of his shoulders.

'Get a rope,' a rabble rouser in the crowd called out.

'Whoa there, Sullivan,' the sheriff rebuked the rouser. 'This fella is Monk all right, but that doesn't mean that we can just string him up.' Loud protestation broke out among the crowd, but the sheriff stood firm. 'There'll be no lynching in my town!'

'Why waste time with a trial, Sheriff,' the galoot from the train questioned. 'The bastard will be hanged then anyway.'

This view was given unstinting backing from the increasingly angry mob.

'Times are a-changing,' the Tonto Crossing

lawman said. 'Law and order is coming. The book kind, with judges and juries. And that ain't no bad thing neither.' He held up his hands to appease the crowd. 'I'll cage Monk. Then I'll send for a US marshal—'

'Why a US marshal?' the trouble-stirrer called Sullivan questioned.

'To oversee fair proceedings,' the sheriff said.

'Make sure you tuck that killer in comfy at night, Tom,' another man angrily shouted from the back of the crowd.

'A US marshal will take time to get here,' Saul Gordon said in a quiet aside to the Tonto Crossing lawman. 'How're you planning on preventing Monk's lynching?'

The lawman sighed deeply. 'I probably won't. But I wear a badge and took an oath that says I've got to try.'

The sheriff's reply raised Dan Stockton's hopes. A jail cell did not appeal to him, but it was preferable to swinging from a branch of the stout oak at the end of Main which everyone seemed intent on stringing him from.

The sheriff's gaze fixed on Saul Gordon.

'Guess you'd do no diff'rent, Marshal?' He asked hopefully, 'Will you be sticking around for a spell?'

Gordon shook his head. 'Got pressing business, Sheriff.'

'Go on home,' Healy ordered the mob. For a

24

brief spell the crowd remained stationary and scowling. 'Go on,' he hollered.

Grumbling, the mob dispersed, except for a small group of huddled men who gathered outside the saloon, casting malevolent glares. It was not difficult to imagine what they were planning. Plans made, they headed into the saloon for the liquid courage to carry them out.

'Inside, Monk,' the sheriff ordered, and honestly told Saul Gordon, 'I don't count you among my friends to have landed me with Cy Monk, Marshal.'

The Tonto Crossing lawman roughly shoved Dan ahead of him. He slammed the law office door shut. He drew his six gun and held it on Dan.

'Cell keys are on the hook by the door leading to the cells, Monk. Grab them.' Dan took the brass keyring from the hook. 'Keep going.' He also added the warning: 'One false move and I'll cut you down.'

There were three cells, all empty.

'The first cell will do just fine. Step inside. Then reach out and lock yourself in, Monk.'

'I'm not Monk,' Dan grated.

'Yeah. Sure you ain't. Just turn the damn key in the lock.'

'By tossing me in jail, you're signing an innocent man's death warrant, Sheriff.'

Dismissive of his protest, Healy left. Dan Stockton lay on the bunk and pondered on how, in the blink of an eye, life could turn so sour.

Darkness came, and a package wrapped in cloth was dropped through the bars of the cell window. Dan picked it up, and felt the familiar feel of a six gun. He hurried to the cell window to catch a glimpse of his benefactor, but saw no one.

Who would want to help him? Or was the messenger a benefactor at all?

A dark thought crept into Dan Stockton's mind. He quickly checked the Colt's chamber. It held six shining loads. He had thought that maybe, thinking that his problems had been solved, the messenger would count on Dan rushing to freedom, only to find that he was running straight into an ambush, holding an empty six gun.

With law and order steadily spreading west, and officers with the fairness and fortitude of the Tonto Crossing sheriff to enforce it, times were changing quickly. Wildcat justice would soon be a thing of the past. However, it took time for men to change, and some still sought and preferred the swift justice of a lynch rope or a bushwhacking, most losing no sleep if their victim proved to be innocent.

Stockton weighed the six gun in his hand. What kind of *hombre* would want to help Cy Monk? And that's who he was, to everyone in Tonto Crossing.

CHAPTER THREE

Tom Healy was dozing in his chair dreaming of Ellie McDonald, the Scots lass all the way from Dundee, who owned the café just a stone's throw from the law office. It was a dream he frequently had. He had not yet made up his mind if his dream about Ellie sprang from desire for the feisty fire-brand, with the strange lingo. Or if it was the wholesome grub she served up at the Happy Belly café. At times, when he had a gnawing in his groin and a hungry belly, he thought about asking Ellie to marry him, and kill two birds with one stone. Then, looking at the Scottish beauty, he'd decide that awake he was dreaming more than when he slept.

'Sheriff!' Dan Stockton's summons jerked the lawman woozily from sleep, just as he was about to kiss Ellie McDonald. 'Sheriff, you hear me?'

'Folk in the next county can hear you, Monk,' he growled. 'What d'ya want?'

'Water. I'm thirsty.'

'I ain't your darn nursemaid!'

'I'd get it myself if I could,' Dan called back.

'Oh, hell,' Healy grumbled, and heaved himself out of the chair. He sniffed the air, closed his eyes and sighed. 'Blueberry pie.'

'Sheriff?'

'I'm coming,' Healy barked.

He picked up the tin cup he had used for his supper, and ran his finger round the inside to scrape off the dried coffee residue. Then he went and filled the cup from a water barrel in the office corner.

In his cell, Dan Stockton strained to hear the movements of the sheriff and to interpret them. When he heard the lawman's steps draw near, he sought the shadows at the rear of the cell. Thankfully, the coal oil lamp in the narrow hall had not been lit. Healy would have to strain to see him, while the light from the office would give him a good view of the sheriff. When Healy entered the cells, Stockton's luck was in. He was not wearing his gunbelt.

Peering into the gloom, the lawman asked, 'Want this water or not, Monk?'

Dan said, 'I keep telling everyone that I am not Cy Monk, Sheriff. But no one listens. So. . . .' The sheriff froze at the sound that came from the shadows – the hammer of a six gun being cocked. Stepping forward, Dan ordered, 'Open the cell, Sheriff.'

28

Tom Healy's bowels rumbled. This was Cy Monk he was facing. When the killer got out of that cell, he'd be a dead man. Maybe not right away, because the killer would want to make his escape in as quiet a fashion as he could. But later he'd come looking. A week, a month, maybe a year or two. But one day he'd look up, or turn round, and Cy Monk would be back for his revenge.

Shrewdly, Dan Stockton guessed the sheriff's thoughts. 'Have no fear, Sheriff. I really am a fella called Dan Stockton.'

Healy was unconvinced. He had chased Monk, almost caught him a couple of times. He'd recognize his dial anywhere, and the feller in his cell was Cy Monk for certain.

'Ain't got the keys on me,' the lawman said.

Dan was knocked back. Of all the possibilities and permutations he had gone over in his mind since the gun was dropped through the cell window, the sheriff arriving without the cell keys was one possibility which had not come to mind. It was on such a turn of bad luck that a man could lose his life.

'I'll go outside and get them, if you want?'

Dan snorted. 'And a six gun too, huh?'

'Can't let you out of that cage if I can't open the door, Mo – Stockton.'

'Isn't that a fact,' Dan groaned.

For a crazy moment, when disappointment set in about being so close to freedom, Dan thought about shooting out the cell door lock, but that would have half the town running for the jail.

'So what will we do?' Healy wanted to know.

The answer to the sheriff's question did not remain a mystery for long. The backdrop of light from the law office vanished. Someone had extinguished the lamp on the sheriff's desk. A bunch of keys clattered on the floor at Healy's feet. The law office door slammed shut. Dan Stockton's grin was a wide one.

'Looks like my guardian angel is working hard to save my hide, Sheriff.'

Sourly, the Tonto Crossing lawman grunted, 'The Devil, more likely.'

'Open up, Sheriff!'

Tom Healy had never lost a prisoner in his twenty three years as a lawman, and starting now was as painful to him as a festering wound.

Dan Stockton now knew why he had seen no sign of his benefactor when he had looked out the cell window. He was crouched under the window, listening. That was the only explanation that explained his latest stroke of good fortune.

Stepping from the cell, Dan ordered Healy, 'Back off, Sheriff.'

'You'll never make it out of town,' the Tonto Crossing lawman predicted. 'You're likely walking into an ambush.'

'And if I stay locked up in your jail, I'll hang. Once enough men get whiskied up, they'll be coming with a lynch rope. So it seems to me that busting out or waiting around is a devil's choice anyway.' Healy tensed as if to spring at Stockton. Dan held the Colt steady, and cautioned, 'Don't do anything foolish. I'll be out of your hair one way or another in a couple of minutes.'

Healy's pride was dented. That made him a dangerous adversary. Dan prayed that the sheriff would act sensibly. Because if he did not, Dan wasn't at all sure that he could pull the pistol's trigger to kill a man in cold blood, even to save his own neck.

Working on the assumption that Healy would try and jump him at some point, left Dan with no alternative. 'Sorry.' he apologized, before he laid the Colt's barrel on the lawman's skull.

Tom Healy's legs wobbled. Dan feared that he would not go down. Each man's skull had a different resistance to a blow, and Dan feared that a second blow might permanently harm the sheriff, if not kill him. Striking the lawman again could make him a killer, no better than Cy Monk.

Healy staggered and grabbed at the bars of the cell door, dazed. He was clearly expecting Dan to finish him off. When he said, 'You just keep quiet, you hear, Sheriff?' Healy was downright amazed.

Dan hurried away. He opened the law office door an inch. He put his eye to the crack. Main was deserted. Light flooded out of the saloon, but other than that, the only patches of light came from house windows. As he passed through those pockets of light to the livery at the end of Main, there would be a risk of detection – a small risk, but he'd prefer not to have any risk at all. However, getting past the saloon would present the greatest danger. The watering-hole was packed, and the odds on someone seeing him were stacked against him.

Also, there was the chance that a town resident might be lurking in the shadows, taking the air or having a smoke before turning in. And behind him, there was the risk of Tom Healy gathering his wits and raising the alarm. And, of course, there was the possibility that once he stepped on to the boardwalk, he would be blasted into eternity.

All-in-all, Dan Stockton knew that his freedom was far from certain.

He had an idea. Dan shut the law office door and hurried back to the cells where, luckily, the sheriff was still in no condition to resist being stripped of his shirt, jacket and pants. They were about the same height and build, and Dan reckoned that he just might be able to pass himself off as Healy. His train conductor's uniform would have made him as noticeable as a saint in hell.

Dressing quickly, Dan went and grabbed the sheriff's hat from a peg behind his desk. The hat flopped down to rest on his eyebrows. No wonder his gun barrel had not dented the lawman's head – there was a lot of it. Dan examined his appearance in the sheriff's shaving mirror and decided that, with the exception of the oversized hat which made him look like a clown from a travelling show, he just might pass himself off to any casual viewer as the Tonto Crossing lawman, for the minute or two that it would take him to reach the livery.

He'd soon find out.

Dan buckled on the sheriff's gunbelt. He counted to ten and stepped outside. The one drawback in his plan to masquerade as Tom Healy, was that he could not slip out. He had to exit boldly. *Why would the sheriff be sneaking out his own door?* would be the question that any watcher would ask him or herself.

No gunfire.

Dan counted his steps.

Still no gunfire. . . .

CHAPTER FOUR

There were two possibilities. There was no ambush. Or he was successfully passing himself off as Tom Healy. Now if the sheriff's hat did not fall down completely over his eyes, he might just find his way to the livery.

He hugged the shadows for as long as he could, letting his eyes get accustomed to the dark. He began his walk to the livery, counting every step. He felt naked in the openness of Main, but using the boardwalk might bring him face-to-face with the surprise he was hoping to avoid. He was halfway along the street.

'So far, so good,' he murmured.

No sooner had he uttered the words, the surprise he feared presented itself.

'Howdy, Tom. Nice night, if the easterly is a touch blowy.'

Dan glanced to the shadowed porch from where the man had spoken.

'Yeah,' Dan answered, deadpan.

Any conversation would reveal that he was not the sheriff.

The mysterious man joked, 'You sure you can see your way from under that hat, Tom?'

Dan laughed, and continued on.

'Ain't very talk'tive t'night, are you, Sheriff?'

The man's displeasure at Dan's moody response to his friendly greeting showed in his tone. But there was also another chord accompanying his displeasure – curiosity.

Dan Stockton tensed. Two men had come from the saloon and were crossing the street at an angle which, at Dan's present progress, would bring them almost face-to-face. Such a close scrutiny would be the end of his charade. And if he suddenly changed tracks, it would only make the man on the porch even more curious than he already was.

Dan slowed his steps, but not noticeably, to keep as much distance as possible between him and the men crossing the street from the saloon. The men were looking his way, and he could feel the increasing scrutiny of the man on the porch, too. He had a sense of entrapment. And a feeling of luck forsaking him.

'Who's guarding that fella Monk, Tom?' the man on the porch enquired. The question stopped the duo from the saloon in their tracks. 'If you don't mind my saying so, it don't seem right to leave a desperado like Cy Monk unguarded, Sheriff.'

'That's right, Luther,' one of the men agreed. 'Sheriff?'

Dan was limping from crisis to crisis, and it was only a matter of time, he supposed, before it became one crisis too many. It looked like he had come to the end of the road for sure. Any attempted bluff by way of explanation would almost certainly unmask him.

One of the men, the taller of the two, leaned forward, peering into the gloom at Dan. Behind him, Dan heard a door opening – the law office door, he reckoned.

'Look at Tom Healy,' Luther hollered. 'Staggering about near-naked, holding his head and wobbling like a Saturday night drunk. But if. . . ?'

'It's Cy Monk!' one of the duo who had come from the saloon yelled, diving for his six gun.

Dan Stockton went rigid. Any second now he would be caught between blasting guns.

CHAPTER FIVE

Stockton's hand flashed to the .45 hugging his right hip, the gun feeling strange and heavy. For the last couple of years, while earning his crust as a railroad conductor, he had had no call for packing a pistol and had become gun-rusty. A while further back in his meandering life, he had been gunslick, and he was now keenly regretting that he had not kept up the routine of practise which he had so diligently pursued before settling for the comfortable and boring life of a railroad conductor.

His thumb snagged on the Colt's hammer, losing him precious seconds. The man who had drawn was those seconds ahead of him, and the second man was not far behind his saloon partner.

'Annie, woman,' Luther called out. 'Sling me my shotgun.'

A wild shot from Tom Healy split the air, but caused no concern. However, shortly, the Tonto Crossing sheriff would have his full senses back and making every shot count.

'Dang it, step 'side you fellas,' Luther hollered.

The Greener roared. The whip of the shotgun's recoil pitched Luther backwards through the open door of the house. As he dived to the ground, the shotgun's load shook the air above Dan's head. The blast demolished a couple of the support beams for the saloon's overhang, causing part of the structure to collapse. A great yawning hole was punched in the clapboard wall of the saloon between the saloon batwings and an upper window. The window shattered and collapsed outwards, taking part of the wall with it, giving a clear view into a bedroom where a large-bellied man was wrestling with a wraithlike saloon dove who was putting up a spirited fight, rebuking the man:

'It ain't natural that way, Mr Benjamin.'

Dan was glad of the diversion, and used the seconds to sprint into the shadows in a crouch. A cry went up:

'Cy Monk's busted out of jail!'

The men rushing from the saloon immediately gave priority to seeking Dan out.

'Knowed we should've hanged the bastard when we had the chance, Healy,' an angry voice charged.

'We still can,' another man shouted.

'There he goes,' a saloon whore shouted, pointing to Dan as he leaped across an alley closer to the livery but still too far away, now that he had been spotted.

40

Several guns opened up. The window of the general store exploded. Deadly shards of glass spun about Stockton, any one of which could have been as fatal as a bullet.

'He's headed for the livery!'

'Barnabas,' Healy shouted. 'Lock the damn gates.'

The bald man who had come to the livery door to investigate the ruckus in the street, immediately obeyed the sheriff's order. The livery gates swung shut. The sound of a heavy bar being put in place sent Dan's hope diving. He was caught in no man's land. Men, angry and vengeful, were closing in on him from all sides.

'No one shoot,' the runtish man who had taken on himself the role of mob leader, said. 'This bastard is ropebait.'

'Hold it,' Healy cautioned, shoving back the front-runners for a lynching. To Dan Stockton, he said, 'The game's up, Monk. Drop the gun.'

'You ain't goin' to do the same stupid thing again, Sheriff, are ya?' the mob leader ranted.

'Yeah,' another man snarled. 'You couldn't hold the critter once. What makes you think you can do it now?'

'String him up now,' the mob chanted.

Tom Healy stood firm for two reasons. He was sworn to uphold the law. And he recalled how his prisoner could have finished him off, and clearly could not do so. Strange behaviour for the notori-

ous killer Cy Monk, who killed for the sheer pleasure it gave him. Maybe, Healy thought, that his
prisoner's assertion that he was not Monk, might
have more than a grain of truth in it?

'I said it before, and I'll say it again,' the sheriff
grated. 'There'll be no mob law in my town!'

Consternation broke out. The mob leader and a
couple of his whiskied-up cohorts shoved Healy
aside. They surged forward, grabbed Dan, and
were hauling him to the hanging tree when the
sheriff rounded on the mob leader and floored
him with a jaw-breaking pile driver. The runtish
man, a practised saloon brawler, rode Healy's
punch and rebounded snarling, biting at the leash
as three men held him back.

'Let him go, if that's what he wants,' Healy said,
his fists balled, his gait the stance of a bare-fisted
pugilist.

'Fighting 'mong ourselves over a cur like Monk
isn't right,' an elderly man, joining the crowd late,
said. 'We're civilized folk, I hope. So let's leave the
sheriff do his job and haul Monk back to jail.'

'I figure it's best if you let us handle this, Doc
Ames,' the mob leader growled, his glance taking
in his cronies.

Ames said, 'Thought you might say that, Burns.
So. . . .' The medico took a Winchester from under
his long coat. 'I figured you'd need help, Tom. You
take your prisoner back to jail, while I tell these
fellers how nasty a gunshot wound can be.'

42

Tom Healy said, 'Obliged, Doc.'

Dan reckoned that his rescue from the hanging tree was temporary. The lynch mob's blood was up, and they would not be cheated of their prize. He put this point of view to the sheriff, and got little change.

'You're reaping the downside of your wayward life, mister,' the Tonto Crossing lawman told Dan.

'You know by now that I'm not Cy Monk,' Dan told Healy. 'If I was, I'd have opened your skull when I had the chance.'

'I've got to think,' the sheriff grunted. 'And that ain't easy with bells ringing in your ears.' He waved his pistol in the direction of the jail. 'Move!'

Dan, bereft of hope, walked back to the jail with Healy in close attendance. Crossing an alley near the jail, a sudden volley of shots rang out high over their heads. A saddled horse charged out of the alley. Though surprised, Dan reacted swiftly. He grabbed the horse's reins and ran with the beast until his pace was right to vault into the saddle. On board the bucking horse, Dan gave it its head and galloped through the crowd, low in the saddle as lead buzzed over and around him.

'That's my damn horse, Monk's on board,' a man swore.

As Dan vanished in the night, guns still flashed. Some men were heading for their horses outside the saloon in hope, but knowing that Dan's lead was sizeable and growing fast. In the dark he could

43

take any of a half-dozen trails outside of town.

His mount tiring, Dan drew rein and calmed the excited stallion. He listened to the silence of the night for the sounds of pursuit, and heard none. Dan's progress from there on was more measured and careful. Night riding held all sorts of risks, and come morning, if the Tonto Crossing posse put in an appearance, he'd need the same kind of fire in the horse's belly that it had had during his escape. He needed some place to rest up. More important still, was the need for his horse to rest.

A short way on he came to a ramshackle cabin, long ago abandoned, but it would have to do. There was a patch of good grass nearby, which the horse was already anxious for. He sat on the cabin's rickety stoop and rolled a smoke. He sat watching the rising moon, and wondered who his benefactor was?

He was sucking the last from the smoke when he found out.

CHAPTER SIX

'Thought for a while there you were set to hang, despite my best efforts.' Stockton, his jaw hitting his chest, gaped at his visitor. Marshal Saul Gordon chuckled. 'You're the most inept jail-breaker I've ever come across.'

Dan raised a dark eyebrow. 'Now isn't that a curious thing. A marshal busting a prisoner out of jail. Doesn't seem right to me.' He fixed narrowed eyes on Gordon. 'The question is, why would you want to do that, Marshal?'

'I need your help to get inside an outlaw roost down near the Mex border called Devil's Pass. Heard of it?'

Dan nodded. 'Well named, too. The men hanging out there are some of the toughest *hombres* in the west. You'd be shot to hell before you ever got close.'

'That's where you come in.'

'Don't see how.'

45

'I figure that they wouldn't shoot Cy Monk and his saddle pard.'

'Now hold it right there, Marshal. Aren't you forgetting something?'

Saul Gordon shrugged. 'Don't think so.'

'I'm not Cy Monk.'

'I know that.'

Dan was stunned. 'You do?'

'Sure do. You see, you've got your right little finger,' Gordon said. 'Last year in a game of black-jack, Cy Monk dealt himself too many aces. One of the men at the table chopped Monk's right little finger off with a tomahawk he'd taken as a trophy from an Indian, when he reached for one pot too many. And that, as you claim, makes you Dan Stockton and not Cy Monk. But just looking at your dial, no one would know it.'

Angrily, Dan said, 'You let me go through hell, and all the time you knew I wasn't Monk!'

'Had to.'

'Is that a fact,' Dan said, sourly.

'Look,' Gordon explained, 'I couldn't believe my eyes when that woman on the train thought you were Monk. Then a plan I've been working on fell right in place.'

'Plan? What plan?'

'The plan that will get you and me into Devil's Pass, sucking air.' He went on. 'Devil's Pass is the hideout for gun-runners, running guns to the Apache. A deadly and dirty trade, you'll agree?'

'Sure I agree, Marshal.'

'And you'd want to do something about it. To save the lives of all those innocent folk who the Indians are slaughtering.'

Wary, Dan said, 'Rooting out gun-runners from Devil's Pass is the law's job. Or the army's.'

Saul Gordon said, sadly, 'Maybe you've got more in common with Cy Monk than your dial, Stockton?'

Dan Stockton shifted uneasily. 'What's that supposed to mean?'

'I thought you were a good and honest man. But if you can turn your back and let that Apache slaughter go on, when you can do something to stop it, I guess I figured you wrong.'

Stockton's discomfort grew under Saul Gordon's glacial glare. The marshal's eyes clouded, and his voice cracked. 'My sister ranched here. Had a good husband and three fine kids, all girls. Nat, Elinor's husband, had his innards ripped out while they watched. But that was only the start of their horror. Elinor had yellow hair. So had her daughters. And you know how partial to yellow-haired women Apaches are. Don't have to draw a picture, do I?'

Dan Stockton felt as low as a rattler on his belly.

Gordon, seeing Dan's shame, said, 'I knew I wasn't wasting my time, Stockton.' He came and sat alongside Dan. 'Now. About my plan. . . .'

CHAPTER SEVEN

'What?' Dan yelped, when Saul Gordon delivered the punchline of his plan. 'Did you say rob a bank?' he checked.

'Not just any ole bank. The Ellsmere Bank.'

Stockton was knocked for six. 'You're loco. Lawmen don't rob banks. And no desperado in his right mind would try and rob the Ellsmere Bank either. Not if he wanted to avoid lead poisoning for sure.'

'Harry Worthton is the badge-toter in Ellsmere. . . .'

'That's why you'd have to be crazy to try and rob the bank,' Dan interjected.

'. . . He's a good friend of mine.'

'Oh, yeah. Did you tell him you're figuring on robbing the bank?' Dan asked, sarcastically.

'Yes.' Dan shook himself, to make sure that he was not asleep and dreaming. 'But we won't be taking any money,' Gordon explained. 'It's a ploy

49

to get us into Devil's Pass. No one has ever robbed the Ellsmere Bank. Word will get out fast, and grease our way into the outlaws' roost to get us close to the gun-runners.

'Though robbing the bank is a set-up, it will have to look real enough, of course.'

'Just how real would that be?'

'Well. . . .'

'Yes.'

'It would have to be convincing. When we bust out of the bank, the law will sling lead our way.'

Dan snorted. 'Will the bullets know that the robbery is a pretence, too?'

'I was going to rob the bank myself. But with Cy Monk along, it'll add that touch of skullduggery to the proceedings that the blackhearted honchos of Devil's Pass will appreciate, don't you think?'

Saul Gordon slapped Dan on the back.

'We should turn in now. Get an early start. If we leave at first light, we should reach Ellsmere about mid-afternoon on Wednesday. It's got to be Wednesday,' he murmured, preoccupied.

'Wednesday or any other day isn't good for robbing banks,' Dan said.

'It's not a robbery as such,' Gordon emphasized. 'About ten minutes before the bank closes would be the best time to rob it. The day's takings will be bulging the safe.'

'Does that make a difference if the robbery is fake anyway?'

'Don't you see? That's the time real bank robbers would rob the bank.'

Dan supposed that that made sense. 'You've really thought this out, haven't you?'

'I surely have, partner,' Gordon said.

'Partner?'

'Well, that's what we are, Dan.'

Dan Stockton fell asleep wondering how, in such a short space of time, his life as a train conductor had done a cartwheel to bank robber. Even if robbing the Ellsmere Bank was only a set-up.

'A darn strange world,' he mumbled, as sleep overcame him.

CHAPTER EIGHT

Ellsmere impressed Dan Stockton. It had a wide main drag that was busy with trade. Its shops were freshly painted and looked prosperous. It was a three-saloon town, two facing each other across Main, and one other, quieter and more select, nearer the end of the street. This would be the town's elite watering-hole. It would have hostesses instead of whores, and the scent would probably be Parisian instead of stale beer and old stogie smoke. Many fine rigs with proudly strutting horses passed along the street, mingling with well-loaded buckboards and freight wagons. The hotels and boarding houses were also well presented. Of course, off Main would be different, as in every other town. There the down-at-heel would find cheap doss houses with bugs so fat from feeding on the unfortunate guests that a fella would be in danger of getting a busted rib or two if they strolled across his chest. Every town had its underbelly. But Dan figured, even Ellsmere's seamy side would probably be superior to the best that many western towns had to offer.

Stockton's gaze finally came to rest on the impressive building that was the Ellsmere Bank. The structure had a crawlspace under it, as had many of the town's buildings. A creek running behind often flooded in winter, and the crawl-spaces allowed the water to wash harmlessly under the buildings on the side of the street nearest the creek. The bank had fine mahogany doors adorned with brass handles and a brass knocker with one of those ugly dials carved on it. Gargoyles, Dan had once heard an educated hombre call one of those ugly critters. Why anyone would want one for a knocker beat him.

'We'll drift in quietly,' had been Saul Gordon's suggestion. 'One rider pretty much goes unno-ticed. More than one turns heads.'

Dan had to concede that Gordon had a point. Western towns were always on guard and suspi-cious of strangers. Ellsmere, being the prosperous town it was, would be doubly suspicious. It had busy stores, saloons and hotels. That would mean a lot of profits going into the bank vault. Sitting temptation.

There had ever only been one bank robbery in Ellsmere. Six men rode in, and six coffins went out. Marshal Harry Worthton and his deputy, a gunslick coyote by the name of Ace Brandon, were one of the toughest law teams around.

Brandon would boast, 'Six seconds. Six dead men.'

'Stop fretting,' Gordon told a nervous Stockton. 'Worthton misses nothing, and I passed right in front of his office. He must know that I'm in town.'

'I'd surely feel a lot less worried if you dropped by and told him we were about to implement that great plan you've hatched,' Dan said, 'just to avoid any misunderstanding, you understand.'

'Nothing's going to happen,' Gordon reassured Dan. 'This whole operation must look like it's for real. Now just mosey along to the bank. Not too fast!' he rebuked, as Dan took a couple of long strides. 'And keep that hat hugging your eyebrows. We don't want anyone shouting that Cy Monk is in town.'

'Fat chance of that, with this.' Dan ran his finger along the false moustache made from the hair of his horse's mane. 'I must look like the fool of the century.'

'Well,' Gordon opined, his grin ear-to-ear wide, 'I reckon it suits you, Dan. I sure hope one of those saloon doves doesn't haul you off to her room.'

As he strolled along the boardwalk with a lazy lope, Dan Stockton reckoned that it had to be his fired-up imagination at work, but he could swear that eyes were on him. But on a shifty-eyed look-see at the folk around him, he saw that they were solely in pursuit of their own interests. So that left him with a question. Because, still unable to shake the feeling of eyes on him, Dan wondered about who was watching him. And more importantly . . . why?

Maybe because he had never before robbed a bank, or even purloined a single dime, his gait was signalling his intentions. Was he being too casual? Or was he being too cautious?

He glanced back to where Saul Gordon was leaning against a support beam of the general store's overhang, as easy in himself as a man after a week in a bordello, for some sign as to how he should proceed in the way an innocent man feeling guilty might. Clearly the marshal was not feeling the tingling feeling of eyes on him, because he visually urged Dan to keep moving.

Stockton strolled on, his eyes sliding towards the marshal's office. The window was vacant, and the door was shut. No sign of activity there. At least that was a relief. His gaze then took in the general layout of the town. He saw nothing to disturb him. So why was the feeling of being watched so doggedly persistent?

All he had to do was step off the boardwalk and cross an alley to the bank. Gordon and he had drawn straws to decide who was going to enter the bank first, and he had drawn the short straw.

'When you're inside, and you get a good look-see, come to the window. When I see you, I'll know

56

that there's no surprises in store.'

'What kind of surprises might there be?' Dan had wanted to know.

Gordon had shrugged. 'Can't plan for ev'rything, Dan.'

'That doesn't answer my question, Saul,' Dan had said.

'Well, there might be a feisty customer for instance, who won't know that the bank isn't being robbed for real.'

Gordon had looked away then, the way a man only telling half the story does.

'And?' Dan pressed him.

'Ace Brandon.'

'Who's Ace Brandon?'

'Harry Worthton's deputy. As treacherous as a rattler in a man's bedroll. Sports pearl-handled Colts, with an itch to use them.'

'Are you telling me that this Brandon fella's not wise to your scheme, Saul?'

Gordon shrugged. 'A secret isn't a secret if the whole darn town knows about it,' he said defensively.

'You know,' Dan had said, 'I think we should shelve this whole crazy scheme right now.'

'If we do that, how're we going to get inside the roost at Devil's Pass? The whole beauty of this idea is that this will be the first time that anyone successfully robbed the Ellsmere Bank. That kind of information will travel faster than the wind, so when we show up knocking on the door of Devil's Pass, the welcome mat will be out for us. Makes sense, Dan.'

'I guess,' Dan Stockton agreed. 'But I'll be damned if I can see the sense of it right now.'

'You want those gun-runners caught, don't you?'

'Sure I do. Gun-runners are the scum of the earth.'

'And ev'ry right thinking man should do his utmost to put them out of business, right?'

'That's so,' Dan agreed.

'Well then, this is a good plan to do just that, Dan.'

On reaching the bank, Dan Stockton had the most awful urge to keep on going. But then he thought about all those souls who the Apache would slaughter with the guns the gun-runners would supply, if he abandoned Saul Gordon's scheme.

He swung in the bank door, quaking in his boots. For all of thirty-one years he had been a lawabiding man, and here he was now about to heist a bank. Sure it was a set-up, and he wouldn't be a real bank robber. But it still didn't feel right. He almost leapt out of his skin when he stood on a loose floorboard that creaked and moved under him.

'Only a loose floorboard, sir,' the bank teller said.

A question which he should have asked Gordon

now sprang to mind. Did the teller know of his plan?

'How can I help?' the teller asked, already suspicious of the dithering man.

In the teller's experience, folk came to the bank with their business clearly defined. He glanced at the shotgun on a shelf under the counter, and wondered if he should grab it. His dilemma was, that if the man was a genuine customer he'd scare the hell out of him and make a fool of himself, and Charles Blackwell, the bank president, would skin him alive. On the other hand, if the man was a bank robber, Blackwell would still skin him alive for not grabbing the shotgun. Some days he wished that he had taken the clerking job in the general store instead of the bank. He probably would have too, but his wife Esther had reckoned that being a bank teller would open the door to Ellsmere society. It had not, and now she blamed him for being *just* a bank teller.

The bank was empty.

Ace Brandon stepped out from behind a stack of hay bales outside the livery. He had been watching the stranger who had just entered the bank with more than a little interest. As yet, he did not have him down to be a bank robber, but he might be one in the making. He looked like a man who was stoking his courage.

The man he was with was another matter.

Brandon had seen him somewhere before.

'Mister?' Dan looked at the roly-poly teller, who had a head as hairless and shiny as a whorehouse mirror. 'Closing in a couple of minutes.'

'I want some change,' Dan said.

'Change?'

'You're a bank, aren't you?'

The teller sighed. 'What do you want change of?'

'A dollar.'

'A dollar?'

'Something wrong with that?'

Exasperated, the teller groaned, 'No.' He held out his hand. 'Your dollar.'

Dan had by now drifted to the window as Saul Gordon had told him do.

'Mister. . . ?'

'Keep your hai – shirt on,' Dan grumbled. 'This is a real pushy bank. I might decide to do business elsewhere, you know.'

The teller's face took on a sour twist. 'I think the bank will survive, if you do.'

On the street, Ace Brandon contemplated his options, and settled for waiting. If the stranger was a bank robber there would be others with him. He'd wait and see who else drifted towards the bank. It came as no surprise to see the gent he thought looked familiar head that way. Brandon searched his mind to put a name to the face, but failed to come up with one.

When Saul Gordon entered the bank, Ace Brandon checked his guns, replacing any missing bullets. He was ready. Any second now there would be a couple of bank robbers lying in Ellsmere's dust.

CHAPTER NINE

When Saul Gordon stepped inside the bank he immediately drew his .45, which Dan thought was a strange move, if the bank robbery was fake. It was stranger still when he growled, 'This is a stick up!' Strange piled on strange when the marshal pulled off Dan's false moustache.

The clerk grabbed the counter to support his jelly legs. 'Don't kill me, Mr Monk,' he pleaded. 'I've got a wife and two kids. I'll do anything you want.'

He was already scooping up dollar bills.

Gordon pulled two cloth sacks from under his shirt and tossed them across the counter. 'Fill them fit to burst!'

The teller grabbed the sacks. 'I'm filling.'

'Toss over the blunderbuss under the counter,' Gordon ordered the teller.

'Yes, sir,' the teller whined, and complied, still stuffing the sacks with his free hand, cursing that he had not reached for the shotgun when he had the chance.

Still reeling, Dan Stockton took time to find his voice. When he did, he asked, croakily, 'What devil's trickery is this, Gordon?'

Gordon laughed. 'That dial of yours sure gets cooperation, Dan. Nice touch, that moustache, don't you think? Served it's purpose. Got you inside the bank without being rumbled.'

Dan's confusion sorted, he said angrily, 'You never had any plan, other than to rob the bank, had you?'

'There you are, mister.' The teller eagerly threw the cloth sacks over the counter. 'They won't take another dollar.'

Gordon grabbed the sacks in mid-air. 'Cover him,' he ordered Dan, and went to look out the window at the street.

Seething, Dan said, 'I'm no bank robber! I don't want any part of this.'

Saul Gordon paused. 'Like it or not you're a bank robber now. And we've got a problem.'

'Problem? What kind of problem?'

'Remember I told you about a feller called Ace Brandon? He's lurking, ready to cut us down the second we step outside. We need insurance, Dan.' Gordon beckoned the teller forward. 'Like a hostage.'

'No,' Dan sternly objected.

'Want to be hanged here instead of Tonto

Crossing? If you're not shot full of holes first!'

The teller pleaded with Gordon, 'Please, mister. Ace Brandon will open up without asking any questions, the second the bank door opens.'

Saul Gordon grunted, 'You've got plenty of packing to soak up lead.'

'Now hold on a second,' Dan protested. 'This whole caper's got out of hand. We've robbed the bank, when all we were supposed to do is give the impression of robbing it. And we're now risking a man's life by taking him hostage.'

Dan glared at Gordon.

'You're no lawman, are you, Gordon? And I've been the biggest fool ever born!'

Grinning, Gordon ripped the marshal's emblem from his shirt and squeezed it in his fist. Dan was taken aback to see the badge crumple up. 'Bought it in a fancy goods store a couple of days ago when I was in a tight spot and needed a masquerade.' He held up the stuffed sacks. 'What're you worrying about. When we arrive in Devil's Pass with this kind of loot, those gun-runners will be only too willing to count us in.'

'Count us in?' Dan yelped.

'Of course.' Gordon chuckled. 'Never saw anyone fall hook-line-and-sinker for a tall story like you, Dan. I figured that the gab about saving folk from the kind of carnage the Indians are wreaking with those rifles the gun-runners are trading for gold, would make an honest Joe like you hopping mad. And that long-legged yarn about the sister I don't have. . . . Well, I knew that would be a clincher. Oh, the part about me knowing Harry Worthton is true, though. You see, Harry's my brother. I'm Jess Worthton.'

Dan cringed. He had just helped one of the territory's most notorious outlaws to rob a bank – the Ellsmere Bank at that! And who would believe that anyone older than a single day would be gullible enough to fall for the yarn he had spun?

'Now the best thing you can do, Dan, is help me and yourself.'

'And how do I do that? The helping myself bit, that is.'

'By throwing your lot in with me.'

'Never!'

'Think about it,' Jess Worthton urged. 'No one's going to believe that you weren't a full and knowing partner in this caper. So ride with me. We can run those guns to the Indians as good as anyone.'

'I don't want a dime of your ill-gotten gains,' Dan growled.

'A couple of months and we can head for South America and live like kings,' the outlaw tempted. 'What d'ya say, Dan?'

'I say stuff your money and your guns!'

'In that case. . . .'

Jess Worthton shoved the teller ahead of him.

Dan had to think fast. He could not stand idly by and see an innocent man gunned down. 'OK,' he said. 'We'll ride together, but we take our chances now. Let the teller be.'

'But why risk taking lead ourselves, if this lump of lard can act as a shield, Dan. Doesn't make sense to me.'

'They're my terms, Jess,' Dan said, grim-faced. 'Take them or leave them.'

Worthton considered his options for a moment. 'I figure I could make it to my horse with this fella stopping lead.'

'Maybe you will at that,' Dan said. 'But two guns blasting are better than one.'

Jess Worthton grinned. 'You know, Dan Stockton. You just might have a point there.' He scratched behind his ear with the barrel of his six gun. 'Thing is, if I let this fine gent here go, how do we get out of here?'

Dan grinned. 'I reckon I might have a plan.'

CHAPTER TEN

Ace Brandon was not a patient man, and he became more anxious by the second when the bank door remained shut. By now he had got word around town about how he figured the bank was being heisted, and men were lining up to extract the maximum revenge on the villains.

One such volunteer asked, 'What's keeping them, Ace?'

It was a question which Brandon wished he had an answer to. 'How the hell do I know?' he growled.

'No need to bite m' head off,' the man groused.

'Then don't ask stupid questions,' the deputy rasped.

Out of the blue, Brandon knew exactly where he had seen the second robber. In a photograph in Harry Worthton's desk drawer. The photograph had been taken in happier times. Harry had a loving arm around his brother Jess's shoulder.

'Wednesday,' Brandon murmured.

'Yes,' the man crouched alongside the deputy said. 'What about it?'

'Harry goes fishing every Wednesday.'

'So?' the man asked, puzzled.

'What better day for his brother Jess to rob the bank.'

The man's face paled. 'Jess Worthton's robbing the bank in his own brother's town? Shit!'

Inside the bank, Dan was thoughtful. 'Maybe we can get out of this without any gunplay.'

Glancing through the bank window at men taking up positions, Jess Worthton said, 'I don't believe in miracles, Stockton. And busting out of this town is going to take one.'

'Well?' Jess Worthton pressed Dan impatiently, as Dan drew his thoughts together. 'What plan?'

When Dan began to prance on the floor, the outlaw figured that the pressure of events had scattered Dan's senses. 'Funny darn time for dancing, isn't it,' he squealed.

Suddenly, Dan stopped his prancing, when his foot found the loose floorboard he had stepped on when he entered the bank all of (he glanced at the wall clock) only five minutes ago, the longest five minutes of his life.

'What's this great plan, Stockton?' Jess Worthton prodded.

Stockton looked Worthton squarely in the eye.

'I've a way out of here, but it's going to cost you, Worthton.'

'Cost me?' Worthton asked warily.

'Every cent in those sacks, that's what it's going to cost you.' Jess Worthton was befuddled. 'If I'm going to get you out of this town with your hide intact, you've got to hand back those sacks.'

'Something's scrambled your brains,' the outlaw growled. 'I'm not parting with a dime of this loot.'

'Then,' Dan said, 'we're going to wait right here, until those gun-happy folk get tired of waiting and come charging with all guns blazing.'

Jess Worthton snorted. 'If that happens, you'd die too, Stockton.'

'Now,' Dan drawled, 'you might think that you're holding all the aces, Worthton. But you're not.'

'Doesn't seem like that to me, friend.'

'You see, Worthton,' Dan said, 'I figure that dying here and now, is better than living with the law dogging my tail as an outlaw, which I'll surely be if you don't hand that money back.' He turned to the teller. 'You'll tell the law what happened, won't you?'

'Sure will,' he agreed eagerly.

Dan turned his attention to Jess Worthton. 'Deal?'

'You tell me your great plan first,' the outlaw haggled.

'After you've handed back those sacks,' Dan said, steely-eyed.

71

Perspiration beading his forehead, Jess Worthton looked out on the street. More men were taking up positions. 'There's a darn army out there now,' he griped.

'Well make up your mind, Worthton. What's it to be? Shoot-out, or money back to the bank.'

After a brief consideration, the outlaw dropped the sacks full of money on the floor. 'Ain't no pot worth dying for.'

'Mighty sensible decision,' Dan said. He picked up the sacks and handed them back to the teller, now totally bemused by the pace and twists of events.

'Now tell me your damn plan to get us out of here with our hides not shot full of lead,' Jess Worthton demanded of Stockton.

'We crawl out on our bellies, that's how we'll get out of here.'

'Crawl?' Worthton yelped. 'Hasn't anyone ever told you that you can get shot crawling as quickly as standing upright?'

Dan grinned. 'Not if no one knows you're crawling.'

CHAPTER ELEVEN

Dan reached down to prise up the loose floor-board, then he yanked up the next floorboard and the one after that and so on until there was a hole in the floor big enough for him to drop through. 'There's a crawlspace under the bank,' he explained to the outlaw. 'We can reach the alley that way, unseen. I'm betting that all eyes will be on the front and rear of the bank. With any luck, we'll be able to just stroll to our horses and be gone before anyone knows we've left.'

The disbelief on Jess Worthton's face slowly changed to belief. A wide grin spread across the outlaw's face. 'You know, Stockton,' he compli-mented, 'this might still prove to be a stroke of pure genius!'

Dan indicated the escape route. 'You first?'

Worthton was magnanimous. 'No, you first.'

Dan sighed. 'And leave you behind to rob the bank all over again? Fool me once, shame on you.

Fool me twice, and that makes me the West's biggest darn fool!'

Dan Stockton had shrewdly assessed Worthton's intentions. His escape route secured, his thoughts were firmly back on the sacks of dollars Dan had forced him to part with.

'It makes no sense at all to leave all that loot behind, Stockton,' he complained.

'It stays put, Worthton,' Dan said, with no hint of compromise.

There was a brief stand-off between the men while Jess Worthton weighed up his options. He reckoned that he could easily outdraw Dan Stockton, but an exploding gun would bring shooters piling into the bank. And even if he made it through the hole in the floor, it would not take a genius to figure out his plan of escape. All-in-all, though it grieved Worthton to have to leave the money behind, there would always be other banks to rob, he consoled himself. But it sure would be nice to put one across on his stiff-assed brother Harry.

'OK,' he growled. 'It's your way, Stockton.' He cast an eye the teller's way. 'What about him? The second we vanish through that hole in the floor, he'll holler loud enough to give Satan a headache.'

'We'll tie him up and gag him.'

'Better if I busted his skull.'

'If I don't want to be a bank robber,' Dan said, 'I

74

surely don't want to be a murderer!'

With the teller bound hand and foot, and gagged, Jess Worthton stood looking down into the dark crawlspace, a sheen of perspiration on his face. Dan reckoned that Worthton's sweat was a sweat of fear. But there was no time to waste.

'Are you going or not?' he growled harshly.

Swallowing hard, the outlaw vanished down the hole in the floor with Dan hot on his heels. 'You be sure to tell the law about what happened here,' he reminded the teller.

The intensity of the darkness at the centre of the crawlspace surprised Dan, but he welcomed it. Deep inside the crawlspace they would be virtually invisible, but as they would near the edge of the crawlspace, the daylight seeping in would make them visible, and they would have to time their exit from the crawlspace into the alley with extreme caution. The need for exceptional care was made crystal clear when a disembodied voice said:

'Ace Brandon said to cut the bastards down the second they show, Ed.'

'What if they come out with their hands up, Larry?' Ed asked.

'The same thing, Ace says.'

Dan began to crawl slowly towards the alley. Jess Worthton, unnerved by the overheard conversation, outpaced him. Dan grabbed him by the legs and held him back. He thrashed about, his eyes wild. Dan had his earlier thoughts confirmed. Jess Worthton had a fear of confined spaces.

'You hear something, Ed?'

Holding him down with a hand clamped over his mouth, Dan calmed the outlaw. 'We'll be out of here in a couple of seconds,' he whispered.

'No, I didn't hear nothin',' Ed said.

'You fellas ready?' another voice asked. 'They can't stay in there all day.'

Larry said, 'You bet we're ready.'

Dan Stockton began to breathe easier. The immediate danger was past, but it was still a long way to their horses. He nodded to Worthton to move forward. 'But easy,' he cautioned. They made steady progress to the edge of the crawl-space, Dan nursing the outlaw along, conscious of every ticking second.

Dan held on firmly to Worthton as they reached the edge of the crawlspace, to prevent him from scrambling into the alley. Slowly, Dan peered out from under the bank. At the top of the alley, the two men they had heard talking were preoccupied with what was happening on Main. The end of the alley at the rear of the bank was empty, or seemed to be. However, there was the chance that whoever had been assigned to guard the rear of the bank had opted for the less, but more effective ploy of remaining out of view, ready to show at the right moment.

'What's happening?' Jess Worthton asked anxiously.

'Nothing much,' Dan replied, absently, his gaze fixed on the crawlspace under the general store across the alley. 'I've got an idea,' he said.

'No!' The outlaw refused his cooperation point-blank when Dan relayed his thoughts to him. 'I'm not going into another crawlspace.'

'It'll bring us out within spitting distance of our horses,' Dan reasoned, but Jess Worthton's head was shaking fit to spin off his shoulders. 'Well, in that case I guess we'd best take our chance on surprising those honchos guarding the Main end of the alley. But, of course. . . .'

'Of course?' Worthton whined.

'That leaves the men at the rear of the alley.'

'There's no one there.'

'Are you willing to gamble on that?' Dan asked.

Stockton watched Worthton's desperation about going into another crawlspace change to trepidation about taking the risk which Dan had highlighted.

Stockton coaxed, 'The crawlspace under the general store isn't half as long, or no way near as dark, Jess.'

The outlaw nodded. Time was short. Jess Worthton's nerves were stretched to breaking point. Picking the second to go was not easy. All one of the men at the top of the alley had to do was turn round, and they would be sitting targets. Dan strained for a sight of any danger from the opposite end of the alley, but could see none.

'I can't take much more of this waiting,' Worthton said, his voice a rusty croak. 'I've to get air, Stockton. My lungs are fit to burst. My pa, who hated me every bit as much as he loved my brother, used to tie me down in the crawlspace when he got liquored up. One time a rattlesnake slithered in there with me and fell asleep right alongside me.'

Though Jess Worthton had lied and cheated, and had done his utmost to make him an outlaw like himself, Dan was moved to pity as tears welled up in the outlaw's eyes at the memory of his father's cruelty to him.

Worthton grabbed at the collar of his shirt as if it was a hangman's noose tightening around it. Insanity glistened in the outlaw's eyes as bright as a fine diamond in the sun, and Dan could see his reason deserting him.

'You've got to hold on, Jess,' Dan said. 'Those fellas will mosey along soon, I reckon.'

Worthton despairingly shook his head. Gasping for air, he said, 'I can't, Dan. Not for a second longer.'

'Just give me a couple of minutes to think,' Stockton pleaded. 'You don't want to be shot to pieces, do you? And that's what will happen if you go charging out there.'

Dan was relieved to see the glint of insanity in Worthton's eyes dim. But he knew that he could not delay any longer, because Jess Worthton's childhood fear would overcome all other fears –

even the fear of being shot dead.

'Want we should try for the general store crawl-space, Jess?'

The outlaw nodded.

Dan Stockton was not a gambling man. But as he bellied out of the crawlspace to cross the alley, he knew he had chosen the gamble of all gambles.

CHAPTER TWELVE

Dan edged out from the crawlspace an inch at a time, ready to roll back under the bank if lead began to fly. Dan rolled across the alley, gritting his teeth as grit and small stones dug into him. He slid under the crawlspace of the general store, and only then dared to draw breath. He glanced back to see Jess Worthton making steady, but slower progress than he had, debilitated as he had been by the fear and anxiety which had gripped him in the bank's crawlspace.

One of the men at the top of the alley rolled a smoke with expert fingers. He tried to light a match on the heel of his boot without success, and threw away the dud match. He fetched another. Dan sweated. If the man turned to strike the match off the bank wall, he could not but see Worthton.

Dan indicated to the outlaw that he should remain perfectly still.

Jess Worthton's fears were back, and full blown.

Dan feared that he would bolt for it. The slightest movement by Worthton would almost certainly catch the man's eye.

Luck smiled on Dan Stockton and Jess Worthton. The other man struck a match which flared instantly. 'If you stop pissin' in your pocket,' the man ribbed his partner, 'your matches will light.'

Crisis over, Dan beckoned Jess Worthton forward. His relief was short-lived when he saw the mongrel. The dog had wandered into the alley behind the outlaw, and was curiously watching Worthton's antics. Dan was about to alert him, but he held his tongue. The outlaw had more fear in him than he could already handle without adding to it.

But if the dog barked. . . .

Jess Worthton stiffened as the mongrel came to sniff at him.

'Keep coming,' Dan urged in a hoarse whisper. Worthton began an inch-by-inch crawl. The dog, curiously watching, paced him. 'Not far now, Jess,' he coaxed.

Just as the dog howled, Dan grabbed Worthton and pulled him into the general store's crawlspace. But had he been quick enough?

CHAPTER THIRTEEN

'What's that damn hound barking at, Ed?' Larry asked his partner.

Ed chuckled. 'Prob'ly a skulking bitch under the store. Shooo, dog!'

The mongrel's bark got more excited by the second, as Dan and Jess Worthton sought the centre of the crawlspace. A stone bounced near the dog, but his interest in the men in the general store's crawlspace was too keen to have legs put under him. If anything his barking got even more excited.

'Mebbe I should mosey 'long an' see what's got that dog so het up, Ed,' Larry said.

Dan Stockton's heart stilled.

'Oh, it ain't nothin',' Ed said.

'Dunno know 'bout that,' Larry said, doubtfully.

'You reckon, Larry?' Larry had finally got his partner interested. 'I'll go look-see.'

The sound of footsteps reached into the crawlspace. Dan wished that it was darker. A cursory inspection might not reveal their presence, but if the man's search was more thorough, there was little chance that they would go undiscovered. Dan had the sinking feeling that his scheme of using the crawlspaces to reach their horses was about to blow up in his face. Because if discovered, the confined space would work against them. All the man would have to do would be to rake the crawl-space with bullets. Or go inside the store and drill holes with lead in the floor.

'Lie perfectly still,' Dan told the outlaw, whose fear was back in his eyes with the ferocity of a cornered animal.

'We're done for, Stockton,' he croaked.

His hand dived for his six gun. Dan grabbed Worthton's wrist and held the gun in the outlaw's holster. 'Don't be a fool,' he rebuked him. 'There's no way we can shoot our way out of here.'

The man's boots appeared at the edge of the crawlspace. His hand rubbed the dog's head. 'Let's see what's got you so excited, fella.' He was down on one knee when there was a crash of glass.

'Holy shit!' his partner swore. 'The teller has crashed through the bank window, Ed!'

Ed's interest in what had got the mongrel's curiosity vanished. He ran back along the alley to join the rush to the bank.

Dan said, 'Let's get out of here before the clerk tells them where we vanished to.'

Rapidly, the two men made their way under the general store and emerged from the crawlspace under the porch steps, which gave them a good view of the crowd gathering outside the bank.

'Get that damn gag out of his mouth!' Ace Brandon commanded.

Seconds now, and the bank teller would spill the beans.

'Run for your horse!' Dan told Worthton.

The storekeeper, who had come from the store to investigate the commotion outside the bank, yelled out when Dan and Jess Worthton came rolling out from under the store and sprinted for their hitched horses across the street. As he vaulted into the saddle, Dan got a fleeting glimpse of heads turning their way. Jess Worthton, his fear of the crawlspaces behind him, was even more agile in reaching leather. Lead filled the air around them. A chunk of Stockton's saddle horn spun upwards past his face. In unison, he and Worthton swung their mounts and fled with bullets chasing them along the street. As the gap opened up between them and the shooters, Brandon and his men ran after them in an attempt to close the gap before it got too wide to make their pistols useless. But the end result of their sprint was to make their gunfire erratic and wild, and it was of little danger to the riders fleeing Ellsmere, as if the devil was chasing them for their souls.

'Get your horses,' Ace Brandon shouted out.

There would, of course, be a posse on their tail. But Dan figured that with the gap between the pursued and the pursuers widening all the time, allied to the myriad trails through the canyon and ravine-dotted country to the south of Ellsmere, their luck would have to hit rock bottom to cross paths with the posse.

'Yahooo!' Jess Worthton hollered. 'We're free and running, Dan.'

Not willing to indulge the outlaw's antics, Dan dampened Worthton's spirits. 'We're not safe until we're right out of this territory. And that will take a couple of days, during which at any time that posse could catch us up.'

'Not so,' Worthton said, but with slipping confidence. 'Not so,' he repeated a moment later, his eyes now constantly checking his back trail.

Dan took pleasure in the fact that he had rattled the outlaw's chain. It was a small consolation for the ordeal Worthton had put him through. As the evening shadows lenghtened, Dan settled on a narrow canyon whose high rockfaces would give the smoke from a fire time to evaporate before watching eyes saw it.

There were other considerations besides the Ellsmere posse to consider. An hour ago he had seen smoke to the east. Thick black smoke, the kind of smoke that might rise from a burning homestead.

Indians, he reckoned.

The canyons, gullies and ravines were welcome routes of escape from the posse. But they were heading into Indian country, and the same canyons and ravines might hold all manner of nasty surprises; surprises that would be much worse than the Ellsmere posse.

Apaches, for instance!

CHAPTER FOURTEEN

Dawn ended a tense night, most of which Dan had spent awake and watchful for both two-and four-legged predators. Darkness had brought safety from Apache attack, but that did not mean that they would not take advantage of the night to creep up close, so that when daylight came they could spring. During the night Dan had heard a couple of animal calls, which might or might not have been genuine. The calls could also come from Indians communicating with each other. Dan Stockton had, during his footloose days after the war, often found himself in Indian country of one tribe or another. But of all the Indians he had crossed paths with, like everyone else who had, he feared the Apache the most. They were fierce, unrelenting fighters, and mercy was not a virtue they practised. Any sane man would give them as wide a berth as he could.

Dan shook Jess Worthton awake. 'On your feet.'

Grumbling sourly, the outlaw curled up. Dan, his nerves raw, was in no mood for Worthton's dallying. He placed his boot on the outlaw's rump and shoved. Worthton was unceremoniously dislodged from his blankets, and rolled on to the canyon's stony ground.

'What the hell did you do that for?' he groused.

Dan had let Worthton sleep on through the night, fearing that if he alerted the outlaw to the possibility of Apaches being in the neighbourhood, his jitters would make a bad lot worse. Dan had chosen to err on the side of caution, and wisely so, he reckoned. Worthton in a lather and shooting at shadows was the last thing he needed.

'Saddle up,' Dan ordered.

'Saddle up?'

'Lying on your ear make you deaf?' Dan growled.

'My sides are meeting. I'm not going anywhere without breakfast.'

Dan, his patience snapping, barked, 'Like to eat it with the Apache?'

Worthton's eyes blazed with concern. His glance went every which way. A rustle in a nearby bush had him diving for iron. Left with no option, Stockton kicked the gun out of Worthton's hand, hoping that he would not pull the trigger in a reflex action. Or that when the gun clattered on the ground it would not go off. Neither happened, but it was a hell of a long second which Dan had lived through. A small animal, scared, skittered from the bush.

'We've got to creep out of here,' Dan rebuked the outlaw. 'And hope that we can slip by the Indians. A tall order when it's the Apache a man is dealing with.'

They saddled up as quietly as they could, and walked their horses for a spell.

'I feel eyes on me, Dan,' Jess Worthton fretted.

'Imagination,' Dan replied, off-handedly. Only he had the same feeling. A cold finger trickled along his spine.

The feeling of watching eyes persisted for most of an hour. Their tension was at a peak when, from behind a boulder, stepped a young girl, ragged and bloodied. This time it was Jess Worthton who stayed Dan Stockton's hand.

'That was a damn fool thing to do!' Dan berated the youngster. 'You could have got yourself killed.'

'Help me, mister,' the girl with hair the colour of ripe corn pleaded, before passing out.

'Where the hell did that kid come from?' Worthton speculated. 'Way out here.'

Dan figured he knew exactly where the girl had come from. He recalled the smoke of the evening before. The girl's home, he figured. He dismounted and set about reviving the girl, drip-feeding water from his canteen on to her parched and cracked lips. Slowly, she came to. Seeing Dan she reacted violently, her hands clutching at him, nails trying to rake his face.

'Easy,' Dan said in a calming voice. 'We're friends.' Her blue eyes wildly scanned the terrain. 'The Indians are gone. Rest.'

He went and got his blanket and laid it on the ground for the girl. He got Jess Worthton's blanket and rolled it in a pillow. The outlaw drew Dan aside.

'How can you be sure that there's no Indians 'round?'

Dan said, 'The girl.'

Worthton looked at the young but well-developed girl with the corn-coloured hair, and saw the sense of Dan Stockton's reasoning. She'd be a trophy that any Indian would want to posssess.

Dan said to the girl, 'Was that your home I saw smoke rising from last evening?' Tears welled up to cloud the girl's eyes. She nodded. 'Are you the only survivor?' Dan wished he could have found the words to elicit the information he needed less brutally, but time was short. Right now there were no Indians in their neck of the woods, but that did not mean that there would not be, and soon.

'Yes,' she said.

Contrary to popular belief, the Apache were careful planners. They would have watched the girl's homestead for a long time before they attacked. Therefore, they would know that she was not among the dead. They would seek her out.

No sooner had Dan thought about this than Jess Worthton voiced those same fears.

'Shut up,' Dan said to the outlaw in a gruff aside. 'The girl is scared out of her wits as it is!'

'She's not the only one,' Worthton flung back. 'Let's hit the trail while we still can.'

'The girl needs to rest.'

'Leave her,' the outlaw stated bluntly. 'While the Indians are busy looking for her, they'll leave us alone.'

'You black-hearted bastard!' Dan swore. His fist flashed to send Worthton tumbling backwards. 'Get out of my sight!'

The outlaw was seething, but his concern for his hide overrode his anger. 'We need each other, Stockton. In this hellish country, two guns are better than one.'

Worthton's argument made sense. But against his better judgement, Dan repeated his order for the outlaw to quit his sight.

'Where the hell is she off to?'

Dan swung around to see the girl walking off on wobbly legs. 'Hold up there,' he called after her.

The girl turned, her face showing the pile of years added to it in the last few minutes. 'He's right,' she said. 'Take me with you and you'll bring a whole heap of trouble on your heads. Besides, I've got my folks to bury.'

'I'll help you do that,' Dan volunteered.

'You're crazy as a loon,' Jess Worthton yelped. 'Hanging around here is just asking to lose your hair!'

Dan swung around angrily. 'I told you to git, Worthton!'

'I'm riding sure enough,' the outlaw flung back, vaulting into his saddle.

'You go with him, mister,' the girl pleaded with Dan. 'With my folks dead, I ain't got nowhere to go to anyway.'

Dan Stockton grabbed the girl by the shoulders and shook her. 'You listen to me, girl. It was God's will that you survived. He has plans for you. And you're not going to throw them back in his face, you hear me? I damn well won't let you!' Tears burst from the girl's eyes and she clung to Dan with the fierceness of a last fall leaf in a storm. He tilted her chin. 'What's your name?'

'Hannah,' she said quietly.

'Hannah what?'

'Kowoski.'

'Say it out,' Dan said. 'Loud and clear.'

A flash of prideful determination lit Hannah's eyes, and she spiritedly declared, 'Hannah Kowoski's my name, sir.'

'Good.' Dan took her hand to shake it. 'I'm Dan Stockton. You can call me Dan, Hannah.'

Hannah smiled, and her face glowed with an inner beauty. She hugged Dan again. 'That will surely be my pleasure, Dan.'

Holding Hannah at arms length, Dan said, 'Now show me the way to your homestead, Hannah. We've got work to do there, before we head out.'

'Head out? Where to, Dan? There's nowhere to head to.'

Dan Stockton's cocky confidence slipped. Hannah had made a good and sensible point. He could not take her along with him.

'You've got neighbours, haven't you, Hannah?'

'The Cords, about ten miles east. And there's the Mooneys to the south.'

'Christian folk?'

'Yes. Nat Cord more so than Mooney.'

'Then I figure that they'll do the right thing and take you in,' Dan opined.

'Take me in?' Hannah's mood became defiant. 'I'm not for taking in, Dan. I can work hard, and—'

'Shush, Hannah,' Dan said softly. 'You're not much more than a child. You can't stay out here on your own. Do you want your folks to keep spinning in their graves with worry?'

Hannah's shoulders slumped in resignation. 'I guess you're right, Dan,' she conceded. 'But who's to say that the Cords and the Mooneys haven't suffered the same fate as the Kowoskis?'

Dan did not want to contemplate that cruel possibility. Because if he did, he had no answer as to what he was to do with Hannah.

'You can ride behind me,' he told Hannah.

Turning, he said to Jess Worthton, 'I figured that you'd be in Mexico by now.'

'If I had sense I would be,' the outlaw flung back. 'But like I said, two guns are better than one. And I don't mind admitting that being on my own with Indians on the rampage scares the hell outa me!'

'Kind of changes a fella's mind about running guns to them, huh?' Dan said.

Jess Worthton hung his head sheepishly. 'Let's get the burying done with, and make tracks out of this country, Dan.'

A while later, on their journey to the Kowoski place, they came upon a smouldering wagon and, though hardened as their wayward lives had made them, Dan Stockton and Jess Worthton paled at the awful sight before them. A naked man was tied to the wagon wheel, scalped and mutilated, his private parts butchered. The face of the naked woman lying near him had frozen in death with the full horror of what had happened to her, before the Indians cut off her breasts and scalped her, too.

Hannah Kowoski screamed. Dan swung round in his saddle to clamp a hand over her mouth, but she leaped from the horse and ran away, her screams filling the surrounding hills until her legs gave out in a faint. Dan cursed that he had allowed the scene of carnage to suck him in the way it had. He should have anticipated Hannah's reaction to the terrible sight.

'Shit!' Jess Worthton swore. 'That catawauling will have every Apache from here to Mexico headed this way.'

Dan was already alongside Hannah. He patted her face and hands. 'Wake up, Hannah,' he urged. 'Sling me your canteen,' he ordered the outlaw.

Worthton grudgingly obeyed. 'Go easy on that water,' he rebuked Dan, as he liberally poured the water on Hannah's face.

'There'll be a well at the Kowoski place,' Dan said.

'I figure there won't be. The Indians will have fouled it. They know that a man in this hell's cauldron without water, is a dead man.'

Hannah spluttered, her eyes opened, rolling. She lay back exhausted.

'Come on, Hannah,' Dan coaxed. 'After all that hell-raising, we've got to make fast tracks.'

With Dan's help, Hannah got to her feet, swaying. As full realization as to why she had passed out registered in her befuddled brain, she swung about to verify the awful scene behind her. Dan stopped her mid-turn. Seeing the Apache butchery once was more than enough for her young eyes, for anyone's eyes. She would carry the burden of what she had witnessed to her old age.

Their mood at its lowest and dourest yet, they rode on to the Kowoski homestead. It would be a day of terrible doings.

CHAPTER FIFTEEN

Dan Stockton smoothed the earth on Rudy Kowoski's grave, the last in a row of five. To his surprise, Jess Worthton had been a willing labourer. Once or twice he had even seen the hint of a tear in the outlaw's eyes, particularly when he laid Hannah's twin sister's violated body in the grave he had dug for her. That had been Dan's second surprise. He had never thought that a man of Jess Worthton's hardcase reputation could have been moved by anything other than his own safety and well-being.

Dark fingers of grey were reaching across the evening sky to snuff out the dying sun when Dan said the prayers for Hannah Kowoski's family. Although he had spoken earlier of God's plan for Hannah, Dan could not see any divine wisdom in letting the Kowoskis travel so far from their homeland to die in the arid territory of New Mexico. Guess it's our destiny to ponder on your mysterious ways Lord, he thought. But you've sorely tested our faith this day.

Throughout the heartbreaking proceedings, Hannah had not shed a tear. But now that the task of burying her family was over, she went off to grieve. Dan was about to go after her to offer his consolation, when Jess Worthton restrained him.

'Let her mourn, Dan,' he said. 'She'll be surrounded by ghosts she'll want to say goodbye to.'

Dan grinned. 'You know what, Worthton,' he said. 'If you're not careful, one of these days you'll find out that you have a heart.'

The outlaw scoffed. But Dan reckoned that the day they'd been through had a whole lot more effect on Jess Worthton than he'd want to admit to. He knew that it surely had had on him.

After a spell, with night closing in, Hannah Kowoski rejoined them. She had changed, seemed older. The child whom Dan had met that morning was gone, and the woman that Hannah would be in the future had emerged.

'I'll prepare supper,' she said, going inside the house.

Jess Worthton's fears rushed back. 'We're not hanging around here, are we?'

'Don't have a choice,' was Dan's reply.

'Travelling by night would keep us safe from those red devils,' the outlaw reasoned. 'Come morning we'd have covered a good part of the ground to that army fort west of here.'

'We're tired. The horses are tired. And if a horse broke a leg, it would leave us stranded and helpless.'

'It might be a risk worth taking, Dan,' Jess Worthton argued.

'And it also might be a risk not worth taking,' Dan countered. 'We'll start out an hour before dawn,' he offered as a compromise.

'Two hours before dawn,' the outlaw countered.

'Two? We might as well leave now,' Dan said, becoming impatient with Worthton's wrangling. 'An hour before dawn,' he repeated.

Jess Worthton's argument fizzled out. It suddenly registered with Dan that somewhere along the line, probably when they went through the floor of the Ellsmere Bank, that the leadership of the duo had passed to him. When they had entered Ellsmere, Dan had been Jess Worthton's pawn and idiot, but they had left on different terms. Dan recalled a saying his mother had, rest her soul. She would say that the events shaped the man.

It had only been a day since Worthton and he had fled Ellsmere. But in that day life had packed a whole lot of danger and misery into it, danger and misery which had irrevocably changed three people. And only time would tell if they had changed for the better or the worse. Dan Stockton would bet on it being for the better.

'Supper is coming up,' Hannah called from the house.

Dan looked to the porch where Hannah was standing in the open door, aproned and cast into shadow by the coal oil lamp lighting on the table behind her, and he figured that the woman he had buried, from whose womb Hannah had been born, was not really dead at all.

Hannah Kowoski, Dan figured, would be just fine.

As they walked to the house, Dan asked Jess Worthton a question he had been meaning to ask since he dropped through the floor of the Ellsmere bank.

'How come that ornery critter of a brother of yours didn't try to nail you back in Ellsmere, Jess?'

The outlaw's smile was a wide one. 'Wednesday. Wasn't there. You see Harry was always a man of habit. He'd get up in the morning and dress exactly as he had every other morning. He'd go to church and always sit in the same pew. Barn dance, he'd dance the same dances all the time. And on Wednesdays he'd go fishing. A man of habit is easy to figure out, Dan.'

Laughing, they went inside the house. The way old partners might do, Dan thought.

CHAPTER SIXTEEN

The plan was to drop Hannah off at the Cord homestead and then head on to the fort to rest up for a couple of days, before again risking the trek through Indian country. The fact that the Indian raids had now been in progress on and off for most of a year, was a fact that embarrassed the fort's officers and men. But it was well known, though seldom acknowledged by those suffering the Apache fury, that the seemingly endless supply of weapons to the Indians from gun-runners in exchange for the yellow dust which the Apache held in low esteem, seeing it only as valuable for the trinkets the women and old men of the villages made, was making the army's task of restoring order to the territory all the more daunting. The success of the raiding parties had swelled the Indian ranks. More braves, added to the new repeater rifles, made the Apache seem invincible, and other tribes were itching to emulate them as soon as they got their hands on the guns from the gun-runners. The hotheads in their ranks preached that the gods were with them, and wanted them to drive every single white-eyes from Indian lands. Triumph heaped on triumph made it seem so to the young bucks, and the not so young warriors. The fear was that an Indian uprising on a large scale would completely overwhelm the army and drive the settlers out, those that survived the slaughter.

About a mile from the Cord place, Dan saw the tell-tale smoke.

'That'll be the Cord ranch, I figure,' Hannah informed him.

An hour later, after a feather-light approach, Hannah's opinion was proven to be correct. From a tree-shaded slope overlooking the Cord home, they could see a black mass of vultures in the yard, their heads bobbing furiously as they fed on the Cord family's remains. The fetid stench that wafted on the breeze churned Dan Stockton's stomach, and had Hannah puking. Jess Worthton just sat silently in his saddle, as pale as milk.

'Guess it's the Moon—'

'No, Dan,' Hannah interjected, determinedly. 'Saul Mooney is a cruel man to his own, and that would make him doubly cruel to me. I'll travel on to the fort with you, if you'll have me along.'

'What will you do once you get there?' Dan enquired.

Hannah Kowoski shrugged. 'Can't rightly say until I get there.'

'My stopover will be brief, Hannah,' Dan warned.

'I'll be no millstone round your neck, Dan,' Hannah promised.

Dan said, 'The fort it is then, Hannah Kowoski.'

A few minutes after leaving behind the carnage at the Cord homestead, Jess Worthton drew level with Dan. 'Where're you headed from the fort?' he wanted to know.

'To Devil's Pass, of course.'

'Huh?' the outlaw yelped. 'Did you say –?'

'Yes, I did.'

'You must be real eager to be dead,' Worthton said. 'Even if you make it through this hell-hole with your scalp still on, the first lookout at the pass will cut you down.'

Dan grinned. 'Dan Stockton would be cut down. Not Cy Monk, I reckon. Maybe this troublesome dial I was born with will do some good.'

'Why?' Worthton asked, genuinley puzzled.

Dan Stockton's face set in stone. 'To scuttle those gun-runners, of course. We've surely seen the end result of their evil trade in the last couple of days.'

Jess Worthton shook his head. 'Well, I'm not going anywhere near Devil's Pass.'

'Didn't ask you to,' Dan stiffly replied.

'The Mex border is only a couple of miles from

that fort. I'm riding like the wind for it.'

'Sounds sensible,' Dan said.

'So why aren't you doing the same?'

'Because,' Dan Stockton said, 'I want to sleep nights. And the only way I'll be able to do that is if I do my darnest to bust up that gun-running outfit.'

'Oh, you'll sleep just fine,' Jess Worthton said. 'The dead do.'

Glancing back to Hannah, who had not yet recovered from the latest and awful sight her eyes had beheld, Dan said, 'Better hold up soon. Rest a spell. Have a bite to eat.'

Worthton did not agree. 'I figure it's best to stay in the saddle. Eat up the miles.'

'Hannah won't last,' Dan opined. 'She's had too much horror and grief placed on her young shoulders.' He turned in his saddle. 'You know this country well, Hannah?'

'I reckon.'

'I'm pretty famished,' Dan said. 'Need to rest up. Know of some place I can do that?'

'There's a creek. Probably dry though. Mostly is unless after rain, which we don't get very often.'

'Shaded?' Dan enquired.

'It isn't easy to creep up on, if that's what you're asking?'

Dan grinned. 'That's what I'm asking, Hannah. You lead the way.' Dan stalled Jess Worthton's budding protest. 'You're free to hit the trail any time you like, Jess.'

'Oh, I'll ride along a while longer, I guess.'

'You're company is welcome,' Dan said.

The creek was, as Hannah had predicted, a rock-strewn duct in the sandy earth, with just an inch-wide trickle of water snaking through it. It took patience, but Dan filled their canteens. A fire was not advisable. The air was clear, and smoke, even a wisp from a small fire, would be seen by watching eyes.

'Jerky and biscuits all right?' Hannah asked Dan.

'They'll fill a hole, Hannah, as good as most things.'

Dan had tied up the horses to prevent them racing for the little water the dried-up creek had to offer. Now he took them one at a time, and controlled their intake to avoid belly trouble. He was watering Hannah's horse when he saw the Apache on the far slope, rifle ready. It was too late to go for his gun. The next thing he knew, he was being shunted aside just as the Indian's rifle cracked. Jess Worthton grabbed his chest, having taken the bullet intended for Dan. As he dropped to his knees, blood draining from his face, leaving in its wake a greyness which told Dan that the outlaw was finished, Jess Worthton squeezed the trigger of his .45. The Indian's face exploded, just as another two Apaches sprang from cover behind him. Dan drew his pistol and double-triggered. One of the Indians dropped face-first on to the stony bed of the creek. The second Dan had winged, but he was still lethal. A rifle exploded behind Dan, the load angrily buzzing over his right shoulder. The last of the Apache trio buckled and fell back into the bushes from where he had come, moaning. Hannah scampered past Dan across the creek and up the far slope. She stood over the fallen Indian, and mercilessly used up every round in the rifle.

'Better to be sure than sorry,' she said, as she strode back past Dan Stockton.

Dan checked on Jess Worthton, but knew the result of his check before he did it. 'Thanks, Jess,' he murmured. 'That was a mighty brave and fine thing to do.'

Hannah was in the saddle. 'There'll be more,' she warned.

Dan knew as much. He draped Jess Worthton's body over his horse and mounted up. 'Pretty good shooting,' he complimented, once Hannah's grief-driven anger tailed off.

'Pa said that everyone in the family needed to be able to shoot straight and fast, if we were to have a chance to survive trouble.' Hannah's eyes filled with tears. 'He wasted his time teaching me. When trouble came I ran away, yellow showing all over me.'

Dan said nothing. There was nothing to say. Time, not words, would heal Hannah Kowoski's scars of guilt. If ever time could.

It was late evening when they reached the fort.

It was crowded with folk fleeing the Apache rampage. Nerves were raw, and fights were breaking out. The soldiers had their hands full with their own problems, and their attempts to keep order were perfunctory. Just ahead of Dan's and Hannah's arrival, troopers had ridden in, if that's what the ragged and demoralized men could be called. Among their number were many wounded. Their dead they had left behind, as they fled the superior numbers and firing power of the Indians.

Dan buried Jess Worthton just outside the fort walls, and then sought out the fort's commanding officer.

'What's bothering you, mister?' Colonel Jack Abraham barked, when Dan stepped into his office. 'If it's help you're needing, forget it,' he added even more curtly.

'I was hoping that you might know of some kind family who would take a young girl under its wing, Colonel.'

'Yours?'

'No.'

'Then how come she's with you?' Abraham made no attempt to hide his distaste. 'Are you one of those men who use young girls, and then dump them when their use is over?'

Another time, Dan Stockton would have taken the Colonel to task, but these were strained times, and the much thumbed Bible on Jack Abraham's desk was evidence of the man's beliefs. Such a man

109

would feel justified in his response to the kind of man he had described, and there were many such men. Dan looked pointedly at the Bible.

'If I was such a man, Colonel,' he said. 'This would be the last place I'd be seeking help.'

Abraham's gaze followed Dan's to the Bible. 'That's a fair point, Mr. . . ?'

'Stockton's the name. Dan Stockton. The girl lost her folk in an Indian raid.'

The fort's commanding officer put down the report he was reading, and gave Dan his undivided attention. 'Stockton, you say?'

'That's my moniker, sure enough.'

The colonel's gaze intensified. 'You look familiar, mister. And I think that dial of yours doesn't match your name.'

'Ever hear of a feller by the name of Cy Monk, Colonel?'

There was instant and furious recognition in Abraham's eyes. 'Begley Creek!' he spat.

'Well, I'm not Monk,' Dan said urgently, when the military man's hand dropped to the butt of his pistol. 'I just had the misfortune to be born with a dial uncannily like Monk's.'

'A great misfortune, I'd say.'

'I'd say it was a downright cross to bear, sir,' Dan said.

Jack Abraham drew his pistol and placed it on his desk within easy reach. 'Prove you're not Monk,' he challenged.

110

Dan held out his right hand. 'Monk got his little finger chopped off down Mexico way last year, dealing from a crooked deck. You can check that fact on that new-fangled telegraph you have here at the fort.' Dan strode to the door. 'Meanwhile, I'll seek out a home for the young lady, Colonel.'

'The telegraph wire is down. Not that it's ever up these days.' Abraham commanded: 'Take your hat off.'

'My hat?'

The fort commander picked up his pistol and aimed it squarely at Dan. 'Take it off!'

'Yes, sir.'

Dan swept the hat from his head.

'Turn round,' Abraham ordered.

Dan did not argue. Arguing with a cocked pistol was an unwinnable argument.

'You can put your hat back on now.'

'Obliged, Colonel.' Genuinely curious, Dan asked, 'What was that hat business all about?'

Abraham explained. 'I didn't know about Monk's little finger. But I did know that he had a bullet crease in his hair that never grew back, after trying to heist an army payroll five years ago. I'll see what I can do for the girl, Stockton.'

Hannah, who was waiting outside the colonel's office with her ear to the keyhole, leaped back as Dan emerged, fizzing with excitement to break her good news.

'Don't need no more molly coddling, Dan,' she

111

announced proudly. 'I've got a job.'

'A job, huh?' Dan cast a disapproving eye over the man with Hannah, dressed in the spivish garb of a gambler or worse, he suspected. 'What kind of job would that be, Hannah?'

The suavely-spoken man looped a possessive arm round Hannah's shoulders and introduced himself: 'Jake Thompson's the name, sir. The manager and owner of the Evergreen Players.'

He pointed to a pair of wagons with that name emblazoned on them. Several hardfaced women were leaning out of the wagons, while a couple of brawny men hung around dissuading any visitors.

'I'm going to be an actress, Dan,' Hannah said.

Dan's gaze fixed on Thompson, whom Dan would bet was a whoremaster masquerading as the owner of a strolling players' theatre. Sure there would be plays performed, but only as a front to cover the travelling entourage's real business. Many towns still had a righteous streak, where the Bible was read, preached, and sometimes inter-preted in an eye-for-an-eye fashion, where men like Thompson and his coterie would feel the full brunt of fervent wrath, should their real profes-sions be known.

Dan said, drily, 'An actress, Hannah? That a fact.'

'Mr Thompson said that I could fit in with no trouble at all.'

Dan eyed the whoremaster with open hostility.

'I'm sure Mr Thompson would hold to his word on that, Hannah. But you're staying right where you are until I can find a good family who'll be willing to take you in and treat you as their own.'

Now unmasked, Thompson saw no further need for pretence. He sneered. 'The girl is old enough to make up her own mind, mister.'

'She's barely fifteen years old, Thompson,' Dan flung back.

'Old enough, I say,' the whoremaster said. His glance went to the three brawny specimens guarding the wagons, now sensing trouble. Dan knew that he was on to a hiding to nothing if he pushed, but what alternative had he. He could not let Hannah walk into the honey trap Thompson had set for her. Sneering, his eyes turning from the men back to Dan, Thompson said, 'I guess that's the end of the argument, mister.'

'Well, now,' Dan drawled. 'I don't reckon it is.'

Dan's fist shot out and flattened Jake Thompson's nose. Blood spurted. The whoremaster shot back over the hitch rail outside Colonel Abraham's quarters. His fall was heavy and awkward. He lay winded and rattler mean.

'What're you doing, Dan?' Hannah wailed.

Two of Thompson's henchmen rushed Dan, with an even bigger and meaner gorilla backing them up.

'Right now, Hannah,' Dan said. 'I'm trying to stay alive.'

'Tear him apart, boys,' Thompson snarled.

The first mountain of man swung a fist that looked bigger than Dan's entire head. Dan was lucky that the man had not taken the time to steady himself, and had swung before securing a firm foothold on the boardwalk, making it easy for Dan to sidestep the pile driver and land a hammer blow on the henchman's jaw, which hurt Dan more than it did him.

The second man reached past the first and grabbed Dan by the shoulders and tossed him effortlessly into the street. Dan landed on his back. His spine rattled along every inch of it. The third man of the killer trio drove his boot into Dan's belly, scattering his wits like straw in a gale.

'Stop it,' Hannah screamed.

'Get in the wagon with the women,' the gorilla who had tossed Dan, growled. He shoved Hannah hard in the direction of the wagon. So hard that she went flying into the street alongside Dan.

'Finish him off,' Jake Thompson yelled.

Dan tried to gather his wits, but there was no time.

'Help him,' Hannah pleaded with the crowd which had gathered, and wasted her breath. She grabbed Dan's six gun which had spilled from its holster and cocked it. 'You stay right where you are,' she commanded the man moving in on Dan.

He laughed, showing the stumps of rotten teeth. He reached down and hauled Dan to his feet.

114

'Which arm d'ya want yanked off first, boss?' he asked Thompson.

'Maybe you should just rip his head off, Ike,' the whoremaster said.

'Good idea,' Dan's tormentor said.

'Mister,' Hannah said. 'I gave you fair warning.'

She fired the Colt. Ike's knee exploded. He yelled in agony, his face turning a dirty yellow as the blood washed out of it. His pain-filled eyes spun in his head.

The man on the porch went for his gun, but his hand froze on its butt as Jack Abraham's pistol prodded his spine.

'Drop it,' the Colonel ordered.

The six gun clattered on the boardwalk.

'This fight isn't any of the army's business, Colonel,' Thompson protested.

'You're on army property. That makes it army business,' Abraham stated unequivocally. 'Besides, I hate uneven contests. If you have an argument to settle, let one of you fellas step forward and face Stockton as soon as he gets his wind back. Man to man.'

The ape on the boardwalk stepped forward, grinning wolfishly. 'You go get the burial detail ready, Colonel.'

Dan staggered to his feet, mustering every ounce of energy to remain upright, but for how long was another matter.

'You teach him good, Benny,' Ike urged his partner. 'Teach him how pricey it is to go pokin' his nose in where it's not wanted.'

Dan circled the gorilla called Benny, taking deep breaths to clear his head and settle his vision. Bets were being waged, not on who would win the contest, but on how long it would take for the gorilla to pulverize Dan.

'Won't last longer than the first haymaker,' one man called out.

A second man, much to the crowd's amusement, joked, 'Benny don't have to hit him. The breeze from his fist goin' past will flatten him.'

The ape lunged at Dan, and he stumbled rather than stepped aside. His strength was returning, but he needed another couple of seconds in which he would have to prevent his snarling opponent from flooring him. He ducked another lunge. His comparative lightness compared to Benny's bulk gave him a temporary edge. But that edge would not last for very long. The ape's swinging fists were getting closer by the second. Dan saw a decided gain in aggravating the man as much as he possibly could, in the hope that frustration would make Thompson's henchman careless. What effect any retaliation which Dan could muster would have, was questionable. It would probably be akin to trying to flatten a mountain with a pebble.

'Now aren't you a pretty dancer,' Dan taunted the man, as he danced away from him, mocking Benny's loping strides.

There was some sniggering in the crowd, until a glare from the gorilla's partner silenced it. Dan saw that his tactics were bearing fruit in the glinting anger showing in his opponent's pebble eyes.

'Don't let him rile you,' Thompson scolded his henchman.

The whoremaster's warning went unheeded, as Benny poked air and his frustration grew as Dan waltzed away from him. Quick as an arrow leaving its bow, Dan ducked under the ape's lunging fists and came up swinging. His balled fist drove into the henchman's belly with every scintilla of force he could muster. Benny doubled over, Dan followed up with a brain-rattler to the side of the man's head. The ape grunted. A lesser man would have folded. As Dan came out of his crouch, Thompson's lackey caught him with a blow harder than any mule kick. Dan spun head over heels. Hannah screamed to alert Dan to roll away as the ape's boot crashed down on his head. He swung his left leg and caught the gorilla behind the knees, whipping the legs from under him. He teetered backwards. Dan swung his other leg into the ape's groin. Howling like a wounded animal, Benny dropped to his knees, clutching his crotch. Dan lost no time in getting an armlock round his neck, and applied pressure to the man's Adam's apple with his thumb. Benny gagged as his breath was cut off. He reached back to grab Dan's head, forcing him to lean back, with the result that his hold on the ape slipped.

The crowd had gone completely silent. They were witnessing the impossible happening right before their eyes. Dan, though a fine cut of a fella, was scrawny compared to the man he was fighting, and no one could have forseen any chance of him overcoming the whore-house bouncer.

Dan knew that he had to maintain his hold on the man. If he lost his grip, he was a goner. Much of his strength had been used up in getting his wits back, and the little he had in reserve was fast draining away with the effort of restraining the ape he was tangling with.

Benny's face was taking on the purple hue of a man running out of breath. Maybe another ten seconds would see him fold. But as his strength drained away, ten seconds would be a mighty long time for Dan Stockton to hold out.

Seeing Dan grimly gain the upper hand with each passing second, the third man of the trio decided to take a hand in the proceedings, but by stealth rather than brawn. He pressed his right hand to his side to activate a device on the inside of his arm, and felt the cold steel of a knife blade slide into his hand.

Stockton, fully given over to finishing off the gorilla he was tangling with, had not the time to worry about his sidekick with his hands more than full. Hannah, too, concerned for Dan's welfare, though she was as angry as a polecat at his intervention to prevent her becoming an actress, had not kept her eye on Benny's sidekick. The explosion of Jack Abraham's pistol brought a sudden lull in the contest between Dan and the ape he was locking horns with. Attention passed to the man on the boardwalk, nursing a hand wound. The stiletto blade was quivering in the boardwalk at the man's feet.

'Thanks, Colonel,' Dan said.

The brief diversion gave Dan the break he needed. First to react, he tightened his hold on Benny until the henchman's eyes were ready to pop their sockets.

'That'll do,' Abraham said, and signalled to two soldiers to drag Dan off Benny.

The ape, grabbing his chance, swung a boot at Dan's groin which did not connect because another soldier side-swiped him with a rifle butt, opening up a jagged scar on the henchman's cheek.

Abraham sternly ordered Thompson, 'Tend to your wounds. Then get out of my sight.'

The sorry bunch had no fight left in them, and did as they were told. A woman jumped from a nearby wagon re-arranging her clothes, and joined the other women in the whore-house wagon. Now Hannah knew why Dan had become so het up about her joining the travelling troupers. Because they were not actors at all.

'Ready to join a good family now?' Dan asked.

'I sure am, Dan,' Hannah said.

'Step inside my office, Stockton,' Jack Abraham commanded, and strode ahead. When Dan entered the colonel's office he already had a map laid out on his desk. 'Ever hear of a hell-hole called Devil's Pass?' he enquired.

'I have, Colonel.'

He relayed to Jack Abraham the misfortunes that had befallen him.

Abraham said with a wry smile, 'Kind of dumb, aren't you, Stockton. Falling for the kind of long-legged yarn Jess Worthton spun you.'

Dan shrugged philosophically. 'What can I say, Colonel. The story sounded mighty plausible the way Jess told it.'

Abraham lit a pipe and puffed for a spell. Then he said, 'I'd lose a lot of men I cannot afford to lose if I tried to storm Devil's Pass. A couple of men with rifles could hold out for quite a time in those canyons. Most lawmen talk a lot, but then find excuses to do nothing. Can't say that I blame them. There's a lot of guff about a super posse to smoke out the scum of Devil's Pass, but again a lot of talk and no action. But. . . .'

He considered Dan Stockton for a long time before he spoke again.

'One man – the right kind of man, might just get inside that fortress. Particularly a feller who—'

'Looks like Cy Monk?'

'I hear that they've got an unwritten law at the

pass, that any man outrunning a posse gets automatic sancturary.'

'So Jess Worthton said. Only I'm not being chased by a posse.' It was Jack Abraham's turn to grin. Dan said, 'I've got a feeling that you've got a plan, Colonel.' He sighed. 'Seems everyone I meet lately has.'

CHAPTER SEVENTEEN

'You've got to make it look good, Stockton.'

In the blistering heat of the afternoon, a mile or so from Devil's Pass, Jack Abraham's words echoed back to Dan as the ravine he was in filled with the sound of angry gunfire. The ten men below the high ridge he was on, were the best sharp shooters that Abraham had. And right now they were proving their worth by spraying Dan with lead, a lot of which was uncomfortably close. But like Jack Abraham had said, it had to look convincing. But singed-eyebrows convincing? The ten soldiers, dressed in civvies, were the supposed posse which the colonel hoped would open up Devil's Pass to Dan.

Abraham figured that the residents of the outlaws' roost always had eyes and ears on the prowl, watching the approaches to the pass. That was the reason for the carefully staged shoot-out which Dan was now engaged in.

Two men broke from cover to get a foothold on the shale track up to the eagle's perch Dan was holding out on. Dan sprang from cover for a split second, defying the hail of bullets coming his way. His rifle spat twice, and the two men tumbled back down the track. It was a well-rehearsed and perfectly staged performance for any observer.

Dan again dived for cover as the air and rocks around him buzzed with lead.

'Of course there's always a chance that if this charade is acted out properly, you'll be unlucky enough to catch a stray bullet.'

'Thanks a bundle, Colonel,' Dan murmured, recalling Abraham's warning.

Another man broke from cover, zigzagging across an open patch of sandy soil, his intentions clearly the same as the men who had gone before him. Dan again broke cover to cut the man down.

'After all this is over,' Dan observed, 'We could take this show on the road.'

After a few minutes more of blistering gunfire, Dan, as arranged, mounted up and rode off helter-skelter with the buckshee posse in hot pursuit, but giving him enough of a head start to be out of range of their blazing guns. Just enough ahead to make it look like one hell of a chase to Devil's Pass.

Nearing the pass, two riders galloped out of a gully to Dan's right, guns blasting at the posse.

'Follow us,' one of the men hailed.

Their fire was wild and, added to the distance between them and the posse, it posed very little threat to Abraham's men. It was to their credit that they kept up a spirited chase, risking a stray bullet. Their breakneck pursuit, to within spitting distance of Devil's Pass, greased Dan's entry into the outlaw community he was about to risk his neck in. The fake posse, led by a grizzled Irishman called Ed Walsh only turned tail when, from high up in the pass, several guns opened up.

Sergeant Ed Walsh said, 'I guess we can report to the colonel that the outlaws of Devil's Pass have put out the welcome mat for Stockton, boys.'

Riding through a narrow canyon inside the pass, Dan thought, *it worked just fine, Jess.* The chase over with, one of the riders who had escorted Dan into Devil's Pass, a scarecrow of a man called Spike Ross, rode alongside Dan. Luckily, as it turned out, Dan recognized Ross, a train robber, from a Wanted poster on the wall of his train conductor's cabin.

'Those fellas really wanted your hide, Cy.'

Dan Stockton's dilemma now was, how well did Ross know Cy Monk? Another problem was, Dan knew very little about Monk, the man. Was he an amiable sort? Sullen? Had he brothers – sisters, maybe? Were his folks alive or dead? What did they do? Were they farmers? Storekeepers, maybe? Dan knew that it was only now his problems were beginning. One wrong move and his stay in the outlaw roost would be permanent.

Ross was sizing up Dan. Was he beginning to have suspicions? Dan knew that he had to say something, and say it fast!

'Spike, ya old hound dog,' he heartily greeted Ross, in what he hoped was genuine Cy Monk lingo. He had never been good at accents but, fortunately, Texan was one of his better impersonations. He had heard that Cy Monk was a Texan. Hopefully, he had heard right. 'Thought the law would have strung you up long 'go.'

Ross grinned, not unpleasantly so for a man with a face that would scare Satan. 'It ain't for the want of tryin', Cy.'

Dan laughed. But his laughter masked deep worry. His brain must have been scrambled to not have considered the fact that in a nest of vipers such as Devil's Pass, he would come across someone, if not many, who would know Cy Monk.

Dan wondered if he was riding a dead-end trail to oblivion.

'Kinda outa your territory, ain't ya, Spike?' Dan said.

Ross eyed him up and down. 'This is my territory, Cy.'

Dan felt a knot in his belly. First mistake. He had foolishly assumed that if Cy Monk was a Texan, Ross would also be.

'Heck, didn't ya shoot a coupla women and a kid

126

down Missouri way?' Dan said, joshingly, recalling one of the litany of crimes on Ross's Wanted poster.

'Yeah, that's true. Me and a coupla hardcases, the Lucey brothers, we was visitin' with a cousin of mine. Got himself hitched to a real beauty. We was on the way home when we came 'cross a town with a bank and a dodderin' sheriff. Seemed a pity to let the chance go a-beggin'.'

Dan chuckled. 'Never one to miss an opportunity, that's you, Spike.'

'Well, I figger a man's got to grab his chances, Cy.'

'I figger that way, too,' Dan agreed.

They were now down to an amble, despite Dan's best efforts to maintain a brisk pace, hoping that once inside the outlaw roost he would be able to stay out of Ross's way as much as he could.

'How's Beth, Cy?'

Beth? Who the hell was Beth?

'Oh, dandy,' Dan drawled.

'Yeah?'

Ross seemed perplexed.

'Sure.'

Ross had now slowed the pace to a crawl, his eyes boring into Dan. 'Dandy, you say?'

Dan would have swallowed if he had enough spittle. But his mouth was as dry as Mojave sand. There was no changing direction now. How the hell could he change direction anyway, when he

127

did not have the slightest idea what that direction might be.

'Yeah. Pretty much,' he said, making a pretence of slouching easily in the saddle, yet having every nerve singing and every muscle coiled and ready to spring into action.

'Kinda hard to be dandy when you're in an invalid chair, ain't it?' Ross said.

Dan breathed a sigh of relief. Ross had thrown him a lifeline. 'You ain't heard, have ya, Spike? Beth ain't in no invalid chair no more. One day last fall, she just stood right up out of that chair.'

'Yeah,' Ross marvelled. 'Ain't that somethin', huh.'

'Sure is, Spike.'

'Ya know, maybe . . . naw. Wouldn't work, would it, Cy?'

'Guess not,' Dan bluffed.

How many more times would the ground open under him? he wondered.

'Naw,' Ross said again, after a long consideration.

Fortuitously, a group of riders joined them, bringing Spike Ross's quizzing to an end. Dan breathed a sigh of relief. The immediate danger to his unmasking was over, but he had learned one stunning lesson from his couple of minutes' conversation with Ross. His trip into the outlaw roost might hold many more surprises and, applying the law of averages, there was no way he could bluff his way out of every trap. Even now, when Ross got to thinking about what had passed between them, he might just realize that Dan had cleverly avoided giving a direct answer to any of his questions.

Once inside the roost, there would not be much time to get a handle on who was behind running guns to the Apache. Dan's eyes came to rest on his hands holding the reins, and the fact that he had all of his fingers. Consciously he drew his hands back to rest on his saddle horn, laying his left hand over his right. It was a miracle that Spike Ross had not noticed that he had all of his fingers. But maybe he was underestimating the outlaw? Maybe he had noticed? And maybe he had cleverly set a trap for Dan to walk into once he was in the roost proper.

Perspiring, Dan almost took off his hat to wipe his brow, recalling just in the nick of time that had he done so, Ross would have readily known that he was not Cy Monk. His little finger he might not know about. But a mark five years old, he most definitely would know about.

The leader of the oncoming riders swung in alongside Dan on the opposite side to Ross, and delivered a stunning order: 'Shoot him!'

'Hold on now, Frank,' Ross intervened.

'Maria's orders, Spike,' Frank said. 'Could be a lawman, or one of them new government secret service agents.'

Ross doubled up laughing.

'Did I say something funny?' Frank growled.

'Heck,' Ross said. 'Take a gander at his dial, will ya. Didn't ya never see Cy Monk afore?'

Dan was pleased with the little shiver that ran through Frank. He hardened his features to granite, hoping that he looked satanically evil and displeasured.

'Never d-did,' Frank stammered.

'Well now ya have, mister,' Dan said, menacingly.

'P-pleased to m-make your acquaintance, Mr Monk,' Frank gasped.

'Mr Monk,' Ross chuckled. 'Sounds kinda grand don't it, Cy.' He addressed Frank. 'Ev'ryone calls him Cy, Frank.'

'Not ev'ryone,' Dan snarled, hoping that he was not overplaying his hand. He looped an arm round Spike Ross's shoulders. 'Only my friends.'

'Darn,' Ross grumbled, 'you wanna be Cy's friend, don't you, Frank?'

'Sure do,' he answered, grinning like a man after his first visit to a whorehouse.

'Then,' Dan said generously, 'I guess you can call me Cy . . . Frank.'

'Mighty kind of you, Cy,' Frank simpered, obviously relieved that he was still sucking air.

Ross asked, 'Hungry, Cy?'

'Enough to eat a steer,' Dan replied.

'Then let's get you hot grub, whiskey, and a good woman.'

Dan laughed. 'Devil's Pass, huh. Sure is a strange name for heaven.'

Riding deeper into the pass, Dan came up short on seeing a skeleton hanging from a stunted tree.

Spike Ross said, 'You'd never believe it now. But that fella was real good looking.'

The men escorting Dan laughed.

'Upset you fellas, I guess?' Dan casually probed.

'A lawman who thought he was smarter than we are,' Frank explained, and then added: 'He got off lightly.'

'Did he think that?' Dan joked.

The riders' laughter hiked, much to Frank's annoyance. Dan figured that he was a man who hogged the limelight, and resented anyone taking it away from him. A dangerous man.

'We were busy that day,' Frank said, 'because some of his friends came to try and rescue him.' His gaze settled on Dan. 'Usually we stake them out, high up. Then we watch as the vultures and any other critter of a mind to, feeds on them.'

'Up to now entertainment wasn't that plentiful round here, Cy,' Ross said.

'Up to now?' Dan asked.

'Yeah. This mornin' a travellin' show rolled in.' He chuckled, and winked leerily. 'Well, that's what they call themselves anyways. The Evergreen Players.'

Dan Stockton's heart lurched. Jake Thompson and his outfit arriving in Devil's Pass, the same

131

time as him, was the unkindest twist of luck a man could have.

Riding past the hanging skeleton, Dan wondered if the outlaws of the roost would be too busy to engage in their usual punishment when his cover was blown, which it would be. Because though he was a dead ringer for Cy Monk, Dan recalled that back at the fort when he had gotten in a tangle with Thompson, Colonel Jack Abraham had called him by his real name. And the only question that now remained to be answered was: would Thompson or someone in the travelling show remember that name?

CHAPTER EIGHTEEN

Dan Stockton was beginning to regret letting his emotions overrule his good sense. Of course gun-runners were the lowest of the low, but him being a dead hero would not advance their demise by one jot. He'd be vulture bait, and they would still be running guns to the Indians. Dan began to long for the quiet life of a train conductor, much more than he could ever have imagined possible when he was doing that job.

Coming out of a narrow gorge, Dan's eyes popped wide. He had heard all sorts of rumours about the roost at Devil's Pass, but nothing could have prepared him for what lay before his eyes. A fertile valley with contentedly grazing cows spreading out from a town, though small, which was a match for many of the towns he had been in. It had the standard main drag with stores and a saloon, and several boarding houses. From time to time all the top guns and blackhearts had hid out in this town, and by the look of things, had not wanted for anything.

The town was the brainchild of one Manuel Lopez, a Mexican bandit who had been unlucky enough to catch lead in the back during a confrontation with a US cavalry patrol while herding rustled stock across the Rio Grande. The bullet crippled him and, as there was no way he could continue in outlawry, he got the idea that if he could not be an outlaw himself, he would provide a safe haven for his former kind, and had set up the roost at Devil's Pass. Now, word had it that Manuel Lopez was a very wealthy man. The price for enjoying the safety of the roost was not cheap. The majority of the roost's guests were bank and train robbers, and the price to remain in the roost until the heat of pursuit died down was half of whatever the take had been. And there was no cheating Lopez. He had eyes and ears everywhere. If an outlaw attempted to fool the roost owner, he quickly and painfully learned how unwise he had been.

Sometimes, top guns were allowed to stay free of charge. Most of them hadn't two dimes to rub together anyway. Lopez reckoned that their presence lent class to the roost, he himself having always yearned to be a fast gun. Their stories, told around a fire at night in the Lopez house, were payment enough.

'I told you to shoot this man. Why haven't you obeyed my orders, Frank?'

The questioner was a flame-haired beauty who had come from the biggest house in town, and must be Lopez's daughter Maria, the issue of a union between Manuel Lopez and an Irish woman who had died in childbirth.

'This is Cy Monk, Maria,' Frank said, by way of explanation and apology.

'Is that an excuse for not killing him? Or a reason?' Maria snapped.

Dan had heard many hair-raising stories about Maria Lopez's hard nature. She was a woman who gave no quarter, and was her father's daughter to a tee.

'Give me your gun!' Maria said to a man nearby. Then she instructed Spike Ross and Frank, 'Move aside, if you don't want me to shoot through you.'

A sweat as cold as Yukon snow broke on Dan Stockton's back. It looked like his stay in Devil's Pass was going to be even shorter than he had expected. Frank had no problem in leaving Dan to his fate. To Spike Ross's credit, he was not as ready to desert him. Dan reckoned that whoever Beth was, she had been important to Ross. He was probably hoping to persuade Dan to influence her in a positive manner to consider whatever proposal he had in mind.

'Darn, Maria. Cy ain't no two-bit interloper.'

'Not quite,' Dan said.

'Huh?' Ross queried.

Dan's bold stare fixed unflinchingly on Maria

135

Lopez. His grin was as fetching as he knew how to make it. 'I reckon that I'm better than most here.'

'Shit, Cy,' Ross wailed. 'You sure know how to rub a girl up the wrong way.'

Dan slouched lazily in the saddle. 'Ya know, Spike,' he drawled, 'that depends on how a girl likes to be rubbed in the first place.'

'Holy shit!' Ross exploded, and swung his horse to distance himself from what he was certain would be gunplay. But to his utter surprise, Maria Lopez laughed heartily. All eyes went her way, because it was the first time that anyone had heard her laugh. Her mood, in the main, was dour.

'Cy Monk, huh?' she said. 'Heard stories about you, Mr Monk. None good. Which gives you a mighty fine testimonial to enter our community here.'

Dan looked to the man wheeling himself from the house in an invalid chair. 'It seems that my daughter likes you, Monk.'

'You reckon?' Dan replied, bolder still.

Manuel Lopez said, 'Maria fell in love once. . . .'

Dan grinned. 'Only once?'

'He didn't treat her right. She cut off his testicles and shoved them down his throat.'

Dan said, 'Hope he had a taste for raw meat.'

Lopez laughed. 'Never said.' His laughter died as quickly as it had begun. 'But then I guess it's hard to talk choking on your testicles.'

'I reckon so,' Dan agreed.

'What should we do with Mr Monk, daughter?' he asked Maria.

Maria's eyes were as green as a spring shoot, but they smouldered like brown Mexican eyes. 'We'll let him stay, Pa. We can always kill him tomorrow, if needs be.'

'Mighty generous, ma'am,' Dan said. 'But just keep in mind that if you're going to kill me, I just hate the taste of raw meat.'

A smile as mischievous as Satan's heart played on Maria Lopez's lips. 'In that case I'll be sure to boil them first, Mr Monk.'

Laughter at Dan's expense broke out, but he was happy enough to join in. He had lived past two defining moments so far. He drawled, 'That'll be Cy, Maria.'

Brief anger flashed in Maria Lopez's eyes. Dan figured that no outlaw had been bold enough so far to call her by her first name. However, her anger faded as fast as it had flashed, and it seemed to Dan, though he might be fooling himself, that his boldness had awakened a fire in Maria Lopez that just might burn with a searing intensity.

Now all he had to do was to be careful not to displease her as that other poor unfortunate soul who had entered heaven or hell with his mouth full, had.

'Come in the house,' Manuel Lopez invited Dan.

This got a mixed reaction from the gathered

crowd, which had steadily grown during Dan's saucy exchanges with Maria, that ranged from outright gawking surprise to outright seething resentment.

'No one gets to visit the Lopezes in minutes,' Ross murmured in an aside to Dan, more amazed than if a miracle had happened right before his eyes. 'Looks like Lopez might be lining you up for a son-in-law.'

Ross shivered.

'Don't know if I'd like to be in your boots, Cy. The Lopezes ain't easy folk to please.'

Spike Ross, along with the other men in the saddle, nearly fell from leather when Dan said, 'Later, maybe, Señor Lopez. Right now I've got my horse to water and feed. Then I reckon an hour or two shut eye.'

He could not afford to hang around. Jake Thompson, the owner of the Evergreen Players had come on to the saloon porch to roll a smoke. He was some distance away, but might just recognize Dan's gait.

'Let's say I drop by 'bout six, señor?'

Breaths were held. When Lopez said, 'That will be fine, Señor Monk,' the crowd was stunned in a silence in which a whisper would have sounded like rolling thunder.

Dan touched his hat. 'Señorita. Señor. Until six o'clock.'

Dan quickly showed his back to Thompson. He

swung his horse and headed back along Main, away from the saloon, counting his blessings that the livery was in the opposite direction. He had dipped into the pot of luck again. How much luck could be left?

CHAPTER NINETEEN

The evening had gone well, and now Dan was sitting on a porch rocker with the beautiful Maria Lopez, whose beauty was flattered by the soft glow of a full moon. To every other man in Devil's Pass, Dan Stockton was the luckiest bastard alive.

Maria was thoughtful and dreamy, the way a woman gets when Cupid is about to sling his arrows. After dinner, Lopez had taken Dan aside and let it be known that his heart was not as strong as it used to be. 'A high price has to be paid for fifteen years of sitting in a damn invalid chair, Monk.' Then he had confided. 'I worry about Maria when I'm no longer around. She's as tough as nails, but she's still a woman.'

Dan had remained silent.

Lopez went on: 'She'll need a man to stand by her. I know my daughter. Maria's got a fire going for you. How do you feel about her, Señor Monk?'

The speed with which events had raced ahead had thrown Dan. He simply nodded to indicate that he felt about Maria how she felt about him. It was an unspoken lie. But what choice had he other than deception. Grisly thoughts of being staked out as vulture bait, or the painful but quicker alternative visited on the last man who had displeased Maria Lopez, were uppermost in his mind.

Two wagons rolled in, their wheels making deep tracks in the earth, indicating a heavy load, a load such as crates of guns.

'Visitors,' Dan murmured. 'This late.'

'Gun-runners,' Maria said.

'Gun-runners, huh?' Dan's heart was thumping loud enough to be heard in Mexico. 'A mighty profitable business to be in. Often thought about going into that line of work, but I never had the *dinero*.'

Dan could not believe his ears when Maria called out to the man seated alongside the driver of the lead wagon. 'Mr Long. I have a business proposition for you. Come here.'

'Yes, señorita,' Long respectfully answered.

Once Long was seated, Maria came straight to the point. 'Cy here would like to become your partner.' Long squirmed. 'That does not appeal to you, Mr Long?'

'I've got no objections to another partner, señorita. But it ain't my decision to make. That would be the boss's call.'

Dan held his breath.

'I can understand that,' Maria said. 'You tell

142

your boss what I'd like to happen.' Long nodded his agreement. 'And tell your boss also, that if Cy,' she took Dan's hands in hers, 'isn't in, you're out. You'll no longer be welcome in Devil's Pass.'

Long touched his hat. 'I'll make your wishes known to the boss, ma'am.'

Dan figured that it was time to do some quiet investigating. Long's departure had been amiable, but his square shoulders and jerky gait said that he was madder than hell, and an angry man was a loose-tongued man.

He yawned mightily.

'Ya know, Maria, it's been a heck of a long day. I guess I'll turn in.'

'Turn in?' Maria yelped. 'With a full moon in the sky.'

Manuel Lopez laughed. 'My daughter is a woman of hot blood, Monk. But, of course,' he winked at Dan, 'that's something you'll get used to in time.'

Dan was not sure why Lopez had taken such a shine to him as a potential son-in-law, but he was not complaining. It was an unexpected stroke of good fortune, which he would gladly accept.

Dan yawned again, even more expansively than he had at first.

Maria said in disgust, 'Ah! Why waste a full moon on a man with no energy.' She stormed off.

'Hope I haven't given offence, Manuel?' Dan said.

143

'She'll have forgotten by tomorrow. A bad combination for temper, Irish and Mexican. Sleep well.' Lopez rubbed his chest and grimaced. 'Tomorrow we will talk again.'

'Sure look forward to that, Manuel.'

Dan stood up, stretched, and let his gaze wander to the store at the end of main where Long's wagons were housed. He strolled stiffly away towards the boarding house he had a room in. Once inside, he quickly made his way out the back door and along the backlots to the store, where he crouched at the window. Luckily, the ill-fitting window frame aided his eavesdropping.

Long was speaking angrily. 'I can tell you, Saul, I'm not looking forward to returning to Thunder Ridge and—'

A cross-eyed drunk staggered from a nearby alley. Dan was forced back into a shadow. If the drunk saw him and hailed him, Long would know that he might have had a listener. Dan cursed silently as the drunk held a long-winded conversation with himself, before staggering back along the alley.

Dan grimaced as the store was plunged into darkness. He went to hurry along the alley in the hope of hearing another fragment of information when the gun-runners passed by, but the drunk's meandering progress ruled that out. However, he had one vital piece of information. The boss of the gun-running outfit was in Thunder Ridge. He had never heard of the town, which was surely now his destination. He had only one problem.

Getting out of Devil's Pass.

CHAPTER TWENTY

Dan Stockton made tracks for the livery, concocting a tall tale as he went.

'Howdy, Mr Monk,' the livery man greeted, an old bank robber who was well past trail riding and whom Manuel Lopez had allowed to stay in the roost on a work-for-grub basis. 'Where're you headed?'

'Señor Lopez says I should do my stint of guard duty.'

The livery keeper chuckled. 'Guess he don't want you in Maria's bed too soon, huh.'

Dan laughed along with him. 'Guess not.'

The old-timer slapped his knee. 'You know, when you're hog-tied to Maria, you'll likely welcome guard duty. Just for the rest.'

'I guess,' Dan said amiably, and began to walk the stallion away from the livery.

'Whatcha doing that for?'

'Easing him out. Picked up a knock in that

helter-skelter posse chase today.'

'Maybe you should take another horse,' the keeper suggested. Dan dismissed the idea with a shake of his head. 'Please yourself,' the old-timer said, huffed at the rejection of his suggestion.

Dan walked the horse along Main, feeling the old-timer's eyes bore into him. It had not been a wise move to upset the livery man. He was tempted to vault into the saddle and ride out, but a departing horse at night would likely rouse curiosity. That was the whole reason for walking the horse until he was out of earshot.

Not far to go before he could safely mount up.

'I've been looking to have a word with you. . . '

Dan froze on hearing Jake Thompson. He slid out of the shadows. Dan's hand drifted towards his .45. Any second now he'd be shooting his way out of Devil's Pass, without a hope in hell of making it. But he was determined that when he was fitted for wings, there would be as many of the roost's hard-cases as he could mange to kill standing in line.

Thompson seemed jittery. Why should he be feeling nervous? He held every ace in the deck.

'Look, Mr Monk—'

Monk?

'I'm really sorry about that misunderstanding back at the fort. No hard feelings, huh?'

Dan was dumbfounded. Obviously, Thompson had not heard Jack Abraham call Dan by his real name.

148

'No hard feelings,' Dan generously confirmed, and slapped the whoremaster on the back.

Relieved, Thompson rubbed his swollen nose. 'You really landed one on me, Monk.'

Dan shook his hand as if it were still paining him. 'Yeah. It hurt. Well . . .' Dan mounted up. ' 'Night, Thompson.'

Dan now had two concerns: Jake Thompson and the livery-keeper. If either one opened their mouth, it would soon become evident that his journey had nothing to do with Lopez business. Also, there was the danger that Thompson, when his nerves stopped jangling, might begin to wonder why the scurrilous Cy Monk had been so het up about him getting his hands on the girl back at the fort. It would be more likely that the real Cy Monk would have struck a price for handing her over.

Once out of town he quickened his pace, but not dangerously so. If he succeeded in making it out of the pass, he'd need a horse that would not fold if pressured. He wished that the stallion had had more rest. But he had a bellyfull of fresh oats, which he had not had in a long time.

On his way into the pass that afternoon, he had been wise enough to note the lie of the rocky terrain, and Dan now prayed that his memory would serve him well. He headed for a narrow ravine that was only spitting distance from the lookout post. His passage through the ravine would be fraught with risks, a lose rock, a spill of shale, a snort from the stallion . . . sound would carry far in the still night. But he was fortunate that the full moon had slid behind a cloud bank. Of course, that might turn out to be a curse instead of a blessing, were it to suddenly re-appear at the wrong moment.

As he progressed as quietly as he could through the ravine, he could hear the two lookouts talking. 'No man deserves as much luck as Monk's had,' one of the men said sourly. 'All of this and Maria in his bed, too!'

His partner scoffed. 'You weren't figurin' on marryin' Maria yourself, were you, Jed?'

'That don't seem as unlikely as you think it is, Art Shaw,' Jed said sourly.

'Ah, hell,' Shaw said. 'Maria will probably kill him like she did her last husband anyway.'

'Yeah.' Dan could imagine Jed's long sigh. 'But a man would die with a smile on his dial after even one night shacked up with Maria Lopez.'

'Yeah,' Art Shaw said, dreamily.

Dan was safely through the ravine, but the most dangerous part was still ahead. The short, open stretch between the end of the ravine and the gap which was the gateway to and from Devil's Pass, was washed in moonlight as it swept from behind the clouds.

Should he wait for the moon to be hidden again? Had he that kind of time'? Or should he risk crossing the open ground directly below the lookout post now? At any time his disappearance from town might be discovered. Maria's humour was a bedding one. If she had not got it under control she might just coming looking for him.

'Well, what's it to be?' Dan murmured, impatient with his own indecision.

He decided to try and make it across the open ground, hoping that his run of luck would hold out just a few minutes longer.

'You see somethin' down there?'

The question was Art Shaw's.

'Where?' Jed asked.

'Right by the gap.'

Dan stood stock-still, praying that the shadow from a nearby ledge was deep enough to hide him. The stallion was restless with his stop-start progress. If the horse snorted he'd be done for.

'Don't see nothin',' Jed said. 'This place is just fulla shadows. Most of 'em ghosts, I reckon.'

'Yeah,' Art Shaw said. 'Real creepy place.'

Dan's relief was palpable as the men took to general nattering again. Cautiously, he edged towards the gap. The minute it took to reach it was sheer agony for Dan Stockton. Clear of the gap, he mounted up, and trusted the stallion to find his own footing.

Dan did not fancy the idea of night riding, due to the multitude of risks involved to man and beast, but what choice had he? By sunup he wanted as much ground between him and Devil's

Pass as he could travel.

Near dawn he crossed paths with an oldster whose mule, pick and shovel told of his profession. Kindly, the prospector shared his breakfast with Dan.

'Ever hear of a town called Thunder Ridge?' Dan enquired of the old man.

'Yep.'

'Close by?'

' 'Bout ten miles south of here.'

Dan thanked him and wished him well. 'Hope you find colour.'

'Hope they don't find you,' the prospector said.

Dan did not bother acting the innocent. The oldster had too many years clocked up for him to be fooled.

'Obliged for the grub,' Dan said.

Dan rode away, headed for Thunder Ridge.

EPILOGUE

Dan Stockton was beginning to think that he'd got it all wrong. Thunder Ridge was a one-horse town, with no ambition to become a two-horse town, and the longer he stayed the more unlikely a gun-runner's headquarters it seemed to be. The thing about eavesdropping was that you could get an entirely wrong slant on what was being said. Lolling on the bed in the cheap boarding house he was shacked up in, Dan was counting the minutes to high noon, the time set for his show-down with his challenger from the Silver Arrow of the previous day. It was unlikely that his challenger would put in an appearance, but then pride prod-ded a man to do foolish things.

Just as the hands of his watch reached twelve, there was a knock on his door. Dan cursed his luck. 'Who's there?' he called out.

'Marshal Cade,' came back the reply.

Dan sighed. More aggravation on the way. Cade

had no doubt come to kick him out of town before any shooting started. 'Coming, Marshal.' But to Dan's surprise, Cade's mood was friendly. 'There's a meeting in my office, Monk. I'd like you to come along to it.'

Intrigued, Dan grabbed his hat off the bed. 'Lead the way, Marshal.'

When Dan stepped into the marshal's office, his eyes popped. Present with Cade were Andrew Collins, Long, the Mayor, and most surprising of all the woman from the train whose accusation had started Dan out on the hell's trail he had ridden.

Long said, 'Mighty slick, you getting out of Devil's Pass, Monk. But you'd better pray that Maria Lopez never gets her hands on you.'

'Why did you hightail it?' The question came from the woman. 'The way Long tells it, you stood to inherit the Devil's Pass roost. Along with a mighty feisty woman, too.'

Dan, now over his surprise, grinned amiably. 'Who killed her husband when she tired of him. A real black widow, is Maria Lopez.'

Andrew Collins was next to speak. 'Long says that you want to throw in your lot with us. That right?'

'It takes a special kind of man to be a gun-runner, Mr Monk,' the woman said. 'Do you think you've got what it takes?'

Dan snorted. 'Ma'am, you don't have to look far or enquire much to discover that Cy Monk doesn't

154

have many qualms.' He chuckled. 'In fact I don't have a single one.'

Dan saw the sweetness of the set-up. A gun-running outfit operating out of a town where the marshal, the mayor, and the town's leading citizen formed the nucleus of the operation. Little wonder that they could function without any serious interference.

The woman said, 'I don't like you Monk. I wished that they had strung you up in Tonto Crossing. However, my friends here can see the merit in having a man with your skills and no conscience on board.'

'I admire their wisdom,' Dan drawled.

'Other outfits are trying to muscle in, and need to be taught a lesson.'

Dan grinned. 'Don't want to blow my own trumpet, but I'm a pretty good teacher.'

Andrew Collins said, 'But don't you ever go near Devil's Pass. I don't much care if Maria Lopez skins you alive. My only concern is that we would be booted out of the roost, and lose the very distinct advantages of the Pass as a trading post if she discovered that we had roped you in. I doubt very much if she'd still want you included.'

'Who busted you out of the Tonto Crossing jail anyway?' the woman asked. Clearly she was the boss of the outfit.

'A *hombre* by the name of Jess Worthton.'

'The outlaw?'

'Yes, ma'am. Sometimes Jess liked to masquerade as a lawman – a marshal in fact.'

'Marshal Gordon, eh.'

'Yes, ma'am.'

'Why did he bust you out?' The question was
Cade's.

'Had this crazy notion that we'd rob a bank, and
use the *dinero* to join up with you lot. Or maybe go
into opposition.'

The mayor laughed. 'Isn't that something,
Hester. You being fooled like that.'

The mayor's laughter died under Hester's
glacial glare. 'Where's Worthton now?' she
enquired of Dan.

'Dead.'

'Good. Are you with us, Monk?'

'Hester,' Dan said, 'I don't know how many times
I've got to tell you that I'm not Cy Monk. I've just
got a dial uncannily similiar to his.' He drew his six
gun and covered the group. 'My name's Dan
Stockton. And,' Dan pulled a document from his
pocket, 'you're all under arrest for gun-running on
the authorization of one Colonel Jack Abraham.'

Cade was quickest to react. His hand was flashing for his gun when Dan's .45 bucked. The rotten
marshal grabbed his chest, dropped to his knees,
and on to his face. Andrew Collins almost got to
the derringer in the pocket of his silk vest, and
paid the same final price which Cade had.

Long and the mayor sprang out of their chairs,

hands touching the ceiling. Dan grabbed the jail keys from the desk. 'Ma'am,' he said. 'Ladies first.' Then, snorted. 'If there was a lady present, that is.'

He ushered the trio to the cells, and was well pleased when he turned the key in the locks.

'Kind of hypocritical, isn't it,' he told Hester. 'Wanting Cy Monk hanged, when you're every inch as rotten as him.'

He swung about at the sound of feet clattering on the boardwalk outside the jail. Dan dived to the side of the door leading from the cells to the office, six gun primed. Three men burst in. Dan ordered, 'Hold it right there!' The men froze in their tracks, puzzled. Dan introduced himself and explained what had happened, ready to start shooting if the men turned out to be cohorts of the gun-runners.

One of the men stepped forward, hand outstretched. 'The name's Cal Flanagan, Mr Stockton. This here is Dan Spooner.' Another man stepped up. 'The feller holding up the door frame is Dan Brady. And we're mighty grateful to you, sir, for ridding our town of a nest of vipers.'

Dan learned about how the ordinary folk of Thunder Ridge had tried to cut out the cancer in their midst, and had paid a big price for their efforts. Cade had forced their hands in set up gunfights.

Two townsmen volunteered to get word to Jack Abraham of the happenings at Thunder Ridge, while others set up a rota to stand guard over Dan Stockton's prisoners. A week later troopers from the fort arrived to haul the gun-runners off to a swift and certain justice.

'Where're you headed, Dan?' Cal Flanagan asked, when he saw Dan riding out of town.

Stockton shrugged. 'Wherever the trail takes me, Cal.'

'You're not going back to being a train conductor, then?'

'Don't know if I could live cooped up in that conductor's caboose any more.'

Flanagan said, 'The new town council we set up have been jawing. And we'd like you to pin on the marshal's star, Dan.'

'I don't know, Cal,' Dan pondered. 'Don't know if I'm cut out to be a lawman.'

'Thunder Ridge doesn't amount to much right now, Dan. But you've given us back our town, and we sure as hell intend to make it grow. For a start we've got valleys and canyons chock-full of wild horses round here—'

'Wild horses?' Dan asked, perking up.

'Please stay, Dan.'

Dan looked at Lucy Flanagan, her eyes radiant with warmth.

'I suppose there's nothing lost in my giving it a try for a spell,' Dan told Cal Flanagan, the chairman of the new town council. 'So, if I'm staying, I'd best return my nag to the livery.'

Dan Stockton rode to the livery under Lucy Flanagan's admiring gaze. There was a spark between them, of that he was sure. And he was determined to fan that spark to a full fire. Roots in Thunder Ridge might not be that bad after all.

Leaving the livery he caught sight of his face in a fly-blown mirror in the keeper's hut. He took off his hat and spat on the palm of his hand. Then he applied the spit to his mop of black hair, and parted it to the other side. He examined the end result in the mirror, convinced that he did not look as much like Cy Monk as he had a moment earlier.

'A man's face doesn't matter much, Dan.' He swung around to face Lucy Flanagan. 'Anyway,' she said, an impish smile on her lips, 'a couple of years with me will put a whole mess of wrinkles in it, and then you'll be wishing that you still looked like Cy Monk.'

As they strolled along the boardwalk to the law office for Dan's swearing in as marshal of Thunder Ridge, Dan Stockton never felt so proud. He reckoned that having Lucy Flanagan on his arm was worth every ounce of trouble he had been through, and a whole lot more besides.

Lucy Flanagan and wild horses. Darn, he'd landed on his feet for sure!

There was an old grizzled harp player in heaven by the name of Yeoville Fancy, and Dan had promised him an outfit called Jackdaw Ranch. One day soon, he'd look down and see it.

But that day had almost not come, because a month later Maria Lopez and a dozen hardcases rode into Thunder Ridge seeking her revenge on Dan Stockton, and to his surprise they had been sent packing by the townfolk who had been given back their town and were determined to hold on to it and build a town that they and their children could be proud to be citizens of.

After Maria Lopez and her henchmen had been taught a stern lesson and fled Thunder Ridge in disarray, Lucy Flanagan said:

'You know, Dan. Maybe we should name the day?'

Dan Stockton had always planned on living his life shackle-free, but he was also discovering that a man changing his mind when the prize was right could be mighty fulfilling.

With the gun-runners out of business, Jack Abraham had the maurauding Indians on the run and the settlers and ranchers were moving back to form a community again. The Indians dealt with, Abraham turned his attention to Devil's Pass and rooted out its canker of rottenness with a zeal that had desperadoes giving the territory a wide berth.

Settled down with peaceful days stretching ahead, Dan Stockton began to rope the wild horses that would fill the pastures of Jackdaw Ranch and build the future for another generation.